THE PATH TO SUCCESS

INSPIRATIONAL STORIES FROM ENTREPRENEURS AROUND THE WORLD

Compiled by
Sandy Forster

Inspired Spirit Publishing
an imprint of Morgan James Publishing, LLC

Published by
Inspired Spirit Publishing
an imprint of Morgan James Publishing, LLC
PO Box 362
Mooloolaba
Qld 4557
Australia
07 5476-5584

Morgan James Publishing, LLC
1225 Franklin Ave. Ste 325
Garden City, NY 11530-1693
Toll Free 800-485-4943
www.MorganJamesPublishing.com

Editor: Marlene Oulton, Bullet Proofers.com, www.BulletProofers.com

For interviews with Sandy Forster for both print and TV, contact -
In Australia: Wildly Wealthy Office 07-5476-5584   info@wildlywealthy.com
In US: Jan Beasley 920-264-7035   info@wildlywealthy.com

ISBN 978-1-60037-479-1

Limit of Liability/Disclaimer of Warranty: While all the stories and
anecdotes described in the book are based on true experiences, some of the
situations and names have been changed slightly for educational purposes
and to protect privacy. It is sold with the understanding that neither the
author nor the publisher is engaged in rendering legal, accounting, or other
professional services by publishing this book. If professional advice or
other expert assistance is required, the service of a competent professional
person should be sought. The publisher and author specifically disclaim
any responsibility for liability, loss or risk, financial, personal or otherwise,
that is incurred as a consequence, whether directly or indirectly, of the use
and application of any of the contents of this book.

To thank you for taking the time to read this book,
Inspired Spirit Publishing would like to offer you a

FREE Success Audio

Listen as International
Prosperity and Success Mentor Sandy Forster
shares the strategies that took her from
welfare to millionaire.

Get your copy of this 45 minute audio now at

www.FreeSuccessAudio.com

Listen to this mp3 audio on your computer or burn
to a CD to use in your car or CD player.

Also, make sure you take the time to visit
each author's website (listed at the end of
each chapter) to receive additional free offers,
information and tips so YOU create more
success in your life.

FOREWORD

Sandy Forster

A re you successful? Do you want to be even MORE successful? And exactly what is your definition of success?

If there was a yard stick to measure it by, how do you know when you've achieved it? And what does it look like when you get there?

First of all, congratulations on making the commitment to add unlimited success to your life! Picking up this book was no 'accident' or 'coincidence.' You are definitely someone who wants MORE in your life, and whether your 'more' is financial freedom, personal happiness and fulfillment, building healthy strong relationships, or simply enjoying good health, you're definitely on your way to getting it when you read the inspiring stories contained in this book.

The first step to achieving success is to be clear about what your 'more' looks like to you. I know that years ago when I was struggling financially and over $100,000 in debt, just having enough money to pay the rent equaled success in my world. Your vision may differ from mine, but it's the process of getting there that unites us.

Of course as I achieved each small success, my vision of what was possible expanded to even bigger and better goals. Today I'm a 'Wildly Wealthy Woman' and my life is full of riches – both personally and financially!

I sincerely hope that by reading the following pages containing moving and motivating stories from some of the greatest personal empowerment leaders in the world, alongside those from everyday entrepreneurs, you too will be inspired to pursue your own dreams.

So, go on! Turn the page and get started on building the life and success you've always wanted.

Enjoy your own personal journey to victory as you follow "The Path to Success."

Contents

From Welfare to Millionaire

Sandy Forster

I gaze out my large windows at my own personal tropical oasis. 2 beautiful acres including a spring fed dam surrounded by trees and manicured lawns. I live in an amazingly beautiful 14 room home only minutes from my favorite beach; drive a stylish silver Landrover Freelander; travel overseas whenever I fancy, attending all the personal development workshops and seminars I want. I take myself and my children on wonderful adventures around the world and have a lifestyle many people adore. I'm a Success Mentor to tens of thousand of people, an international speaker, a bestselling author and internet marketing expert!

As I write this, I feel a sense of gratitude flood my body as I gaze upon the family of wild kangaroos and their joeys feed on the lush green grass of my property and reflect on my journey over the past 5 years from welfare to millionaire.

After my husband left me with a 6 month old and 3 year old, I lived in constant struggle for many years. I was working seven days a week in my clothing business which I no longer enjoyed, had over $100,000 of debt and was surviving financially through welfare. My future looked bleak and to say I was stressed about money was an understatement.

My entire life revolved around money or, more precisely, the lack of it. Money consumed me; frustrated me, annoyed me and scared me, and it most definitely eluded me. When it came to creating wealth, I felt powerless, hopeless, useless and worthless. I knew deep down inside I was a good person, so why was my life such a shambles? What had I done to deserve this? "What was wrong with me?!"

Then I discovered there's a secret to getting everything you could ever want in life. It's really simple; in fact, it may be something you have heard about, or understand already. There is a law, a Universal

Law, which states, "We attract whatever we choose to give our attention to – whether wanted or unwanted." The result of this law is this: if you continue to focus on the lack and limitation in your life, you will continue to create and attract more lack and limitation. If you instead focus on the wealth, abundance and prosperity that is already present in your life – no matter how small it may currently be – then you will instead begin to create and attract more wealth, abundance and prosperity.

For some people, this comes naturally. For others (like me), this can be a slow and arduous journey. Through my many money failures, mistakes and unwise decisions when it came to practical money-making steps, I have been fortunate enough to develop a passion for 'what makes people rich.' It is through this passion that I have been able to create my own incredible wealth, and now, share these secrets with people across the globe.

My first thought was, "Okay, just focus on prosperity, wealth and riches, then that's what I'll attract." However when you're raising 2 small children on your own, have $100,000 of debt, making $15,000 a year and constantly can't pay the bills, keeping your focus on abundance is NOT an easy thing.

However, you have a choice as to where your energy or attention is focused. You can choose to focus on what is working in your life and what you want more of, or you can choose to focus on what isn't working and what you don't want. Either way you get more of whatever it is you focus on.

I adore sharing everything I know with anyone who will listen – including my children, constantly telling them, "What you focus on becomes your reality." When I was in my stage of attracting money, but it was flowing out just as fast, my daughter would say, "Blah... blah...blah. We don't need a lecture about that spiritual stuff, it doesn't work anyway! We've still got no money."

And that was the truth. We were still struggling financially even though I was saying my affirmations and visualizing what I desired a couple of times a day. The problem was, the rest of time I was seeing bills and feeling my solar plexus tighten. I was experiencing fear, worry and panic about where the money would come from, that I would never have enough, that I would be struggling forever.

I had to stop and look at what I was creating for myself when my daughter. who was around twelve at the time, came to me the day before her school dance and said, "Mum, I need some new shorts for the dance."

Now I need you to really get this picture – I was having a really tragic week financially. I'd had a check bounce, a few bills had come in, including a red-letter bill (those scary ones), and I was beginning to go into my usual panic mode around money.

So the conversation went a little like this…"Can you buy me my shorts and shoes? I really need them!" "Darling, I don't have the money right now." "You never buy me anything; I have to have them!" "Darling, I said I don't have the money." "Can't you just put it on your credit card?"

The credit card was up to the limit, so that wasn't an option and by this time I'm starting to freak out. I am seething with all sorts of very negative, very strong emotions. Frustration, because even though I was making good money, it was disappearing; embarrassment, because I felt so hopeless at managing my money; guilt, because I felt like a bad mother for not being able to buy things for her; sadness, because I knew how disappointed she would be because she'd be missing out once again and anger, because she was asking me for something I just didn't have. Unfortunately, anger was winning, and the picture was not pretty.

The veins on my temples were throbbing, my eyes were bulging out of their sockets, I was hissing through gritted teeth, had spit flying out of my mouth and I'm sure there were traces of steam coming out of my ears as I screamed like a banshee going to war, "I don't have the money to pay all our bills! I've got to try and pay the phone bill before they cut it off. We just don't have the money –

don't you understand? We're broke right now! WE DON'T HAVE ANY MONEY!"

She looked me squarely in the eye and in all the wisdom of her twelve years upon this earth said to me in her most disgusted tone, "Well, if that's how you FEEL whenever you think about money – the Universe is NEVER going to make us rich."

And I felt like someone had just punched me in the stomach. In that moment, plain as day, I could see why I was still struggling financially. I was attaching my strongest emotions – all negative – to the one thing I wanted most. And in doing so, I was repelling it. I was pushing money away. I was making sure it didn't stay long enough for me to enjoy.

My emotional outburst was not about having money; it was about NOT having money. So 'not having money' was the dominant vibration or energy (or order), that I was sending out to the Universe day after day. And the Universe was picking up that 'not having money' order and giving it straight back to me, day after day.

I was blessed to be shown that although I thought I was focusing on the prosperity I desired, I was actually focusing on what I didn't want, and so kept re-creating it over and over. Since that fateful day, by changing my focus and cultivating a 'Millionaire Mindset', I have gone on an amazing journey from marketing a personal development course to becoming a Life Coach, to creating a number of highly successful coaching and mentoring businesses which focus on showing others how to create a life filled with prosperity, abundance, success and happiness.

I have gone from welfare to millionaire through doing what I LOVE. I show others how they can do the same. By doing what makes your heart sing, the way will be shown, opportunities will arise, contacts will be made and you will tap into that limitless flow of success and prosperity. I teach people world wide how to tap into that limitless stream of abundance and success through the metaphysical AND by applying simple practical strategies.

What was my biggest challenge – relentless money struggle – turned into my biggest opportunity – teaching you how to be wealthy, abundant and RICH beyond your wildest dreams! I offer free resources at www.WildlyWealthy.com and show others across the planet how to be Wildly Wealthy FAST though live teleconferences, seminars and workshops and generally get to spend my days 'playing' at what I love. Life doesn't get much better that that.

The best thing is, I share my knowledge with conviction – knowing that although I had no great education, no money behind me, no connections and no real idea what I was doing, simply by persistently and consistently visualizing, affirming and focusing on what I DID want, I have been able to create a life I love.

Remember, no matter what life throws at you don't give up, keep focusing on what you DO want – because if I can do it, anyone can – including YOU!

Sandy Forster is an International speaker, Millionaire Mindset Mentor, Bestselling Author, Award-Winning Business Owner and mother of two beautiful children. Sandy has a passion for showing others how to create a life filled with richness, prosperity, success and happiness in an easy to understand, empowering and extremely fun way! Visit her websites today for your own FREE prosperity resources - www.WildlyWealthy.com and www.SecretMastermind.com.

Do Something Worthwhile Everyday That Makes You Feel Uncomfortable

Cherry Maclean

Several years ago, my husband, Ian was working at an isolated mine thousands of miles away. Speaking long distance, on the phone with my sister one day, she asked 'Do you want your marriage or not?' Two weeks later I hopped on a plane with our toddler. I told Ian only two days before, so that he could meet us at the airport and ensure we had accommodation. Otherwise I would have added some extra excitement with more of a surprise visit.

A year later with a young toddler at home in the mining town and a second new baby, I started volunteering at our local community center. We already had many successful ladies evenings, but nothing for men. I came up with 'Blokes Astronomy Night' and asked Ian to help as he had a passion for astronomy. Several weeks later we repeated the same event, this time 'Chocolates Under the Stars' Astronomy Night for the ladies, as a result of public demand. I had stepped out of my comfort zone, doing something new, this gave me much more confidence and self-esteem.

Shortly after this I found myself nursing my mother in our own home, without the usual community support, because the mining town was very isolated. She had suddenly become terminally ill and was bedridden. I cared for her every need, 24 hours a day. During this delicate time, I also organized babysitting for our children and got help from local church volunteers to look after my mother, both at the same time, even though my husband was home. I was then able to attend college one night a week to achieve my Computer qualifications. After several months, she tragically lost her fight with cancer. I not only lost my mother, but my best friend too! I continued to attend college, even though I was still grieving, and managed to graduate a short time later.

Then I became the ICT (Information and Communication Technology) Support for one of the largest schools in Northern Australia, making sure all the computers and the network kept functioning. Although faced with problems everyday, I found them to be exhilarating challenges. My previous career was in Office Administration. I'd never thought of myself as knowledgeable enough to take on such a responsible role. I started the computer course for fun, knowing it was important to look after myself, as no one else was. I assured myself that to take time out to look after me was the best thing that I could do for my family and myself, and I would be a better person for them too. The change was scary and uncomfortable, but I took a leap of faith and believed in myself enough, that I would learn the skills quickly and be competent in this new career.

During this time, my eldest boy had being bullied for 3 years at three different educational institutions. When I returned to the workforce in the Computer Support role, I thought he would be okay in a new school, but while working my new job, I was spending a lot of time helping and encouraging him to keep going to school. I saw him punched in the back while I sat in the back of the classroom, after the teacher advised me that there were no bullying problems! He just didn't want to go to school. I talked to the school yet they forgave the bully. I asked many times for my husband to help, but he wouldn't. He didn't have the skills or know how to deal with it, at the time. As a result, the help and support that I felt I should have, wasn't forthcoming.

For the first and only time in my whole life, I fainted from exhaustion in the playground at my son's school. After this, my way of thinking dramatically changed, on a very deep level. My direction in life then became very independent from that of my husband. I really got the message of how much on my own I was at the time. This was a big turning point in my life, realizing how much of my life was up to just me.

Walking home from work, often quite late at night, was an interesting challenge. I had to keep a keen eye out for wild angry buffalo, which roamed our streets at night after the shops closed. However, it didn't stop me, as the walk was very invigorating and gave me time to think and refresh myself. I thought about how overweight I was after having two children. Then I became ill with a stomach virus. It was such a tough strain that a friend was hospitalized from it. I took off several pounds in the next few days. Instead of making up for it by eating extra food, I saw this as an opportunity to continue the weight loss. I proceeded to lose around 2 pounds a week over the next several months, reaching a total of over 44 pounds. I discovered that adversity can show us roads to success, as being ill led to my eventual weight loss which was a blessing in disguise.

I spent many late nights scouring the Internet for inspiration and came across Sandy Forster talking about her book 'How to be Wildly Wealthy Fast' before it had been named. I watched and waited. Then I saw her speak on national television. I knew that I had to be part of this support program. I joined, paid in full, and then told my husband afterwards! I knew if I told him first, I would never have joined. He made all the usual cynical comments that would normally crush me and take away any joy in it, but I was already totally committed. He soon got to like me being in the program.

After a couple of years, Ian also benefited from the extra inspiration, high spirits and new knowledge that I had. He used to think that every person he saw driving an expensive car was a crook. He now feels worthy of success and knows that honest people can make lots of money and live life with the highest integrity. He has become very motivated and is excelling in his own entrepreneurial adventures. We started what is now one of the largest Astronomy Club's in Northern Australia. Ian writes scientific articles for several publications and has his own Educational Astronomy website.

Now a mother to three wonderful children, helping them study has propelled me along a fulfilling journey of children's education. I spent many hours researching educational worksheets and embedding links to the best websites on the school computers. Now I create online educational products. This is something I never would have dreamed of doing a few years ago. Changing my career, participating in The Wildly Wealthy Women's program and doing things that are uncomfortable have opened up many new opportunities.

I now know that if you ever feel powerless and stuck in circumstances. Start by doing something worthwhile everyday that makes you feel uncomfortable, after a while you will see a shift in your belief structure. That's when the real changes happen. It doesn't have to be different everyday, even if it's the same thing for twenty days, as long as it's worthwhile.

Cherry Maclean is an Innovative Designer, Developer and Producer of Children's Online Educational Products, including Fun and Creative Educational Worksheets, Interviews that Kids can listen to from Experts, Science Experiments and much more.

Download Free Educational Products at www.onlinekidslearn.com. For Cherry's Favorite Recommendations on many areas of life, visit www.CherryMacleanRecommends.com.

More info on Cherry is at www.CherryMaclean.com and contact her at CherryMaclean@mac.com, or write to Cherry Maclean, PO Box 440, Edge Hill, Queensland, Australia, 4870.

Trust in Your Inner Weirdo

Jacqueline Johns

I'm a bit of a weirdo.

Since I can remember, people have presented me with their problems. Soon after the introductions, I often hear "I don't know why I'm telling you this, but…" ("Tell me a secret" is tattooed on my forehead!) Hence, I've morphed into "Jacqueline Johns, Life Mentor."

This didn't just involve getting a haircut, a new outfit and erecting a sign. Nooooooo! This morphing was a long, slow process, testing my resilience, resolve and persistence. Because I knew I was put on this earth to help people, I persisted through the very slow start to my business when others would have given up the ghost. Many distractions were presented which could have thrown me way off course, but didn't. Why didn't I give up? How did I know I was meant to help people?

I had help. Help from a resource many people choose to ignore. It's a resource I've introduced to many friends and some (not all) clients. It's what I call the 'Inner Weirdo!'

You may call it God, the Universe, the Force, Divine Spirit, Guides, Angels, Higher Self, Buddha, Allah, whatever. It doesn't mind how you address 'it' (you could even try sitting down tonight and asking for help from your inner weirdo!). Whatever you feel and believe is right for you, is fine. Just know it's there to help you – ask and you shall receive. After asking, be alert for the answers that will come.

The following true stories illustrate how I was kept on the path to Life Mentor.

As I do not wish to influence you in the naming of your divine help, I will henceforth refer to mine as Inner Weirdo (IW). In twenty years when you're playing Trivial Pursuit and the question is "Who coined the term Inner Weirdo?", remember you heard it here first!

Weird Stories That Kept Me On The Path

1. Flicking through the classifieds, my attention was arrested by an advertisement (almost as though it was flashing red) for an expensive Life Mentoring Course. Intuitively, I tore it out and stuck it on the fridge. Whenever I saw that ad, it "buzzed" me, saying "Come on! Do something about me." I couldn't ignore my gut feeling, so I took my first step on the path.

2. Lacking resources to start my business, I asked Inner Weirdo for more clients so I could advertise. IW didn't send clients for whatever reason (there's always a good one), but I did win $1,000 which helped!

3. After many months with few clients, waning resolve and needing some inspiration, I picked up a book which had previously been very inspirational, and said to IW, "I'm starting to lose faith. Can you please tell me if I'm on the right path? Am I meant to do this work?" Limited space prevents me reproducing here the whole answer I received. The last sentence of the page-and-a-half to which I was directed (though I could barely read it through tears of gratitude) read, "You will learn the joy of service, a service that asks nothing for itself but only to uplift others." (*Teachings of Silver Birch – edited by A. W. Austen*) (See my website for full version of answer).

4. A clientless service business is expensive, with overheads etc., so numerous people suggested I locate my office at home. Not an ideal scenario for me, as I predicted possibly attracting fruitcakes, and wished to protect my family. So I set about attracting a rent-free office! What's that? You don't believe there is such an animal? Neither did those closest to me, until I found one! I simply asked IW for help, and the right person - and office - materialized!

5. There were times between clients when I said, "Okay IW, I understand I may not be ready for a deluge, but if you don't send me some dribs and drabs, I'll have to shut up shop." Sure enough, a drib or a drab appeared within days.

6. I hold meditation classes in my waiting room. One day, opening the door to my office from my waiting room, I was shocked to see the floor to ceiling mirror on my office wall totally fogged up! I'd been in my office well over a year and to my knowledge this had never occurred before! At my exclamation of surprise, Donna, the lady waiting for her meditation class, came running in. At the top of the mirror were three perfect circles, as though someone had drawn them in the fog. We exchanged puzzled glances, and I said to IW "If this is a sign, thank you and can you please make it a bit more obvious so there's no doubt?" We completed our meditation, after which Donna jumped up and opened the office door. "You got your sign - there's a heart on the mirror!" I didn't believe her until I saw it with my own eyes! A perfect heart in the fog on the mirror!! Anybody who knows me will tell you I'm mad about the heart shape. My jewellery is heart shaped, my home is full of hearts – I'm just a hearty lady! There is no more fitting sign for me than a heart. Imagine how astounded we were – and still are, when we recount that story! I'm just glad Donna witnessed it, and she saw the heart first, otherwise I may not believe it myself. I was told three times that week that circles mean success (yep- I'm acquainted with other weirdos, too).

7. This story isn't career-related, but is too beautiful to omit. Driving down my street, I observed a white-haired old man struggling along, dragging two large suitcases behind him, one in each hand. As I approached him, I knew IW wanted me to offer him a lift. I drove on until a bend in the road concealed me from the old man, stopped the car and said to IW "I know you want me to give that man a lift, but I can't do it. I don't know what he's got in

those suitcases. My family would never forgive me if I got killed and you can't just go around trusting everybody." As far as I was concerned that was the end of the story, but before I could take my foot off the brake, the words came back "'Trust me to look after you." So, lamb-like, I reversed back up the street, picked the old man up and drove him home. I know those words I was given were not just about that incident. I have taken them to heart and I *know* I'm being looked after, permanently.

Trusting in my Inner Weirdo has guided me to make a successful career from a natural gift. I have been fortunate enough to assist others in changing their lives, learning "the joy of service, a service that asks nothing for itself, but only to uplift others", and my gratitude knows no bounds.

Know that your life can be what you *choose* it to be. Know that there are many resources available to help you along your path, but above all, get to know your own Inner Weirdo!

Jacqueline Johns loves life, (and has the laughter lines to prove it!). She has spent most of her adult life marinating her two children in love, and since they are almost done, has turned her attention to the global population. In Melbourne, Australia, she provides one-on-one mentoring to a Happy Life. Globally, www.HappyLifeMentoring.com provides free info on achieving a Happy Life, and an online service should you so desire. Contact Jacqueline at info@HappyLifeMentoring.com.

I've Been Rich, I've Been Poor. Rich is Better.

Mary King

"I've been rich, I've been poor. Rich is better." So said Sophie Tucker, Mae West and Gertrude Stein, who all eventually became wealthy in their own right.

Few women are financially free. Most rely on a partner, a family, an employer or the government for their income. Unfortunately, most women will find that at some point in their life they will experience poverty. This is a shock to many because it is not generally how we foresee our lives; not the life we would consciously choose for ourselves, our mothers or our daughters.

Some women have learned how to be wealthy; some have learned how to become financially independent. Some women have learned to work only part-time and become millionaires. You can too. Wherever you are now, you can get there from here.

Let me tell you a little about my life. After qualifying as a pharmacist, I married and had five children. We lived in a house with a tennis court and had a life that looked sensational – from the outside. Without going in to detail, my life as I knew it, shattered in a split second. My husband was gone and I was forced to stand on my own two feet. Many painful, happy, challenging, productive and often frustrating years later, I found myself alone and broke.

While living in my brother's beach house, I started to write my first book. For more than a year I'd attracted no paying work. For months I had been feeling the pressure of lack of finances and it weighed heavily on me. Applications for pharmaceutical positions had attracted no response at all. I had to do something.

On June 30th, I did a budget. I had registered a company several years previously for a pharmacy that was now, like most everything else in my life, gone. The company still owned two apartments, both mortgaged, and the cash flow was seriously stagnant. I discovered the company would survive as long as I bought no food and paid no rent. Fine!

The next day I endured humiliation as I stood in line at the welfare office to see what benefits I could get to keep body and soul together. When I told the supervisor how dreadful I felt, he smiled and said, "Sooner or later everyone ends up here." These words somehow made me feel a little better and also motivated me to make welfare dependency avoidable.

I believe there is no such thing as mistakes. Standing there in the welfare office, feeling a jumble of relief and shame, a call came on my cell phone. I admitted my humiliating circumstance to my friend, and she said, "Oh no! You should have resisted."

Immediately a bell rang in my head. Years earlier I had learned, *What You Resist Persists*. I realized that by asking for help I'd stopped resisting poverty. When I arrived home that evening a pharmacist called offering me work. Once I stopped resisting my situation, the energy changed and I was once again 'in flow.'

In less than five years I went from welfare to wealthy, owning property to the value of more than a million dollars.

I've been rich and I've been poor. I can assure you rich is better.

If you simply take the time to learn how to be wealthy you too can become a millionaire. Put money to work for you so you don't have to work for money. When you respect money, it will respect you. I have learned to love money and I believe money loves me.

It wasn't always like that. I grew up taking on my parent's beliefs about money. Some of the money messages I inherited were: "Money doesn't grow on trees." "If you have a lot of money you must have got it by illegal means." "You have to work hard for money." "Money is the root of all evil."

With these messages in my head it's no wonder I was broke!

Maybe you have in your mind messages that are not serving you. It is important to uncover your money pattern, because whatever you think manifests in your life. These beliefs can be deep seated. If you think, "I don't have enough", the result that shows up in your life will be lack of funds.

I decided it was time I chose my own messages. There are a lot of wealthy people on the planet, and surely they were marching to a different money message. I made up money messages that created different outcomes from my parent's messages. Now I believe "Making money is easy." "Money creates freedom and joy." "I now have the skills to make money effectively." "The more money I have, the more I can have."

As a pharmacist I learned to apply formulas. There are formulas for making and growing money as well. Money follows certain laws, so I set up a money system.

Divide your after-tax dollars. Pay yourself first. Take 30% off the top and live on the remaining 70%. The first 30% is divided into three parts: 10% is for investing (Freedom), 10% for savings and 10% for charitable donations. When you are successful with 30%, you can increase it to 50% and start a 'Play' Account and 'Education' Account.

Universal Principles to Grow Your Wealth:

A principle to apply is **multiplication by division**. Sounds odd, doesn't it? Consider that iris bulb you dig up to divide each year and you get the idea. Similarly with money, each segment grows.

Another principle is **mass attracts**. Start with one dollar; add another dollar, the mass increases and attracts more. Before long more money is in the pot.

It is compelling fun to **put money into a Freedom Account** every day. I happily go without a cappuccino and I take a sandwich from home for lunch. I'd rather buy another property with the money I save.

Apply the principle of **leverage** (doing more with less). With the deposit from my Freedom Account and borrowings from the bank, I bought another apartment. The rental covered the monthly repayments. As real estate values escalated the property price increased. By leveraging the increased equity in the property, I bought more properties.

Blow the **Play Account** money each month on fun or luxury. It makes you feel good to splurge on a massage, a special dinner or a new pair of shoes.

Use the **Education Account** to increase your knowledge. Be a life-long learner.

Give to **charity.** Twice in my life I was given quick lessons when I gave to charity. Once while on vacation with my husband and five young children, we listened in church to a petition for a worthy cause. My emotions were stirred. I dug deep and contributed $10. (In those days $10 was a lot of money for us to give away.) Later that day I put a dime into a poker machine and $10 fell in to the bowl. Another time I gave away a large note. Shortly after, the exact amount appeared on the pavement and I picked it up. These experiences taught me not to be afraid to give to charity. Money (energy) goes out and money (energy) flows in to fill the void.

Now I love to share what I've learned via my books, CD's and Rich is Better – Wealth for Women workshops.

Mary King is an international speaker, pharmacist, wealth coach, psychotherapist, author and financial freedom mentor.

Mary is passionate about empowering women and showing individuals how to be healthy, wealthy and become financially free.

Visit her website www.Wealth4Women.net to subscribe to her monthly newsletter giving useful tips and information on wealth, and download for free *10 Proven Steps to Have Your Dreams Come True*.

LIFE DESIGN WITH IMPACT
PILOTING YOUR BRAIN TO CREATE YOUR DREAM LIFE

Caron Egle

I wake up every morning and say "Thank you." My body floods with gratitude as I thank the universe for my wonderful life, my beautiful husband, my children, my family and friends, my work, and my lifestyle. I feel truly blessed to be living the life I have, but it wasn't always that way.

16 years ago I left my first husband when my three children were 1, 2 and 3 years old. I had no job; I was on welfare with no car, and a massive debt having just bought him out of the family home to keep a roof over my children's head! There were times in those early days when I had to borrow money from friends to buy bread and milk at the end of the week. It was not great!

I clearly remember hitting rock bottom when I absolutely owned that I had created everything in my life through my thought process, and I was not happy!! I went into a proverbial tailspin because while I could own that I had created everything, I had no clue at that point what to do differently to have a different outcome. Fortunately, this in itself set up a momentum for change, as I began to dream and create my possible future.

Now, I live the life of my dreams. I am married to the most amazing, wonderful man who still makes my heart skip a beat, even after nearly 10 years together. We have an amazing blended family – a "Brady Bunch" scenario - with our six children. We are building our dream home in the country, and have a magnificent holiday home in the mountains. We travel overseas for vacations, drive a luxury car and most of all we are healthy and happy. I run my own company, IMPACT Learning and Development, and I truly love the fact that I am assisting other people to live the life of their dreams. And life just keeps getting better and better.

Is there any secret to this success? Yes and no. In my work with clients, both in individual coaching, therapy and in training seminars, I come across people every day who are seeking to develop their lives to be more aligned with their dreams. Nobody ever wakes up in the morning and says to themselves, "I want to be less today." We are continually striving to be more.

To more fully understand how to create the life we desire, it is useful to understand how the brain works, and how to harness this in combination with the Law of Attraction to achieve the outcomes we desire. When we understand how our brain functions and how to pilot it, we are empowered to create the life we choose.

How our brain works

Our brain is a magnificent organ which enables us to accomplish, both consciously and unconsciously, all the tasks and functions we need in our lives. The brain is involved in every activity we undertake.

We input data from the environment via our five senses. Csikszentmihalyi (1991), in his book, "Flow", states that humans input approximately 2 million bits of information per second. This amount of data is overwhelming, so our brain filters it by deleting, distorting and generalizing data. We filter this through our experience of:

- time, space, matter and energy
- the language we use (the cup is half empty or the cup is half full)
- our memories
- the decisions we have made
- our personality
- our values, beliefs and attitudes

This provides us with our unique experience of the world. However, these filters can also prevent us from achieving our potential because of our negative self-talk or our limiting beliefs developed over time.

Developing the knowledge and skills to control our internal processing enables us to pilot our own brains in a proactive and empowering way and achieve the results we desire. I teach people about new ways of thinking which includes:

- having an outcome focus rather then problem focus (focusing on what you want, not on what you don't want)
- asking "How can I?" rather than "Why can't I?" questions.
- framing failure as feedback, which we can then act on to change
- looking for what you can do rather than what you can't do or the constraints of a situation
- relaxing and trusting the universe that it will provide from an infinite supply

Understanding the Law of Attraction

Piloting our brains to achieve our results is directly linked to the Law of Attraction. Creation first occurs on the mental plane through thought, and then next on a physical plane. All creation has two phases – mental then physical. Einstein stated that "Imagination is more important then knowledge. It is the preview of life's coming events." What is really important to having the life we desire is to focus on what we want, not on what we don't want. Whatever we put our focus to we create, so our life to date is a result of the past thinking that we had. Life is a continual process of recreation. If we are not getting the results we want, then we need to do something different.

I remember clearly one weekend when the children were on an access visit with their biological father. I had previously written my long, long, long list of attributes of my perfect partner and put it away, letting go of my attachment to form. I allowed myself to have exactly what I wanted. I was sitting on my lounge with my eyes closed and I was truly focusing with every cell in my body the feelings of having it all – of being in relationship with my perfect partner – what I would see, hear, feel, say and do – I was really there! I had such a sense of comfort and gratefulness. Very shortly after that I met my husband – and it is even better than I imagined!

Unfortunately, most of us have limiting beliefs which can hold us back from achieving our life desires. Often these beliefs are very unconscious – we don't even realize we have them. If we haven't gotten the results we desire, then most likely there are some limiting beliefs holding us back – remembering that we are where we are today because of our past thinking. In my work I utilize a range of Neuro-Linguistic Programming (NLP), and TimeLine Therapy* techniques to teach people to remove limiting beliefs at the unconscious level and to firmly entrench evidence based goals in their future.

It is important to remember that we do not have to design and create the life we desire alone. We can seek out a mentor or coach to assist us. All elite athletes embrace the skills and knowledge of a coach to assist them to reach their highest potential. A good coach will help you clarify your purpose, values and goals. They will also provide ideas and questions to support you to take the appropriate actions to confront your habitual, unconscious behaviors and patterns that can be holding you back from achieving what you truly desire in you life. Coach's hold you accountable.

We all have the power to create our life by design. We just need to be really clear about focusing on what we want and be truly grateful as it unfolds before us.

Caron Egle is the managing director of IMPACT Learning and Development. She is a dynamic facilitator, coach and teacher with a unique ability to optimize the desired outcomes of individuals, groups, and organizations through utilizing innovative thinking, learning and coaching strategies. Her vision is to help transform the planet. Caron offers readers a range of free products to pilot your brain and design your life at www.LifeDesignWithImpact.com. Caron can be contacted at caron.egle@LifeDesignWithImpact.com.

You Too Can Find, Flaunt and Fulfill the Goddess in You

Danette Hibberd

It is difficult for many women to recognize the need for change. For so long, I was cocooned in my comfort zone, content to simply drift along each day, with all that was familiar to me. Happy to work for someone else ten hours plus each day, only to go to bed at night and wake the next morning to do it all over again. However, uninvited and unexpectedly, that all changed.

In just a matter of seconds, an accident resulting in three breaks to my spine, altered my life. Following surgery, I spent months lying on my back and my days of enjoying physical activities of aerobics, dancing and having a wonderful time all suddenly stopped. So too, did those jobs that come like second nature to women such as doing housework, cooking, laundry and the weekly shopping. I tell you, it takes something like this to make you realize just how fragile the human body is, and also what it takes to come out at the other end of the tunnel. And, there IS ALWAYS light at the end of the tunnel, and not necessarily that of an oncoming train!

I also learned the value of having the ability (or inability) to do all those mundane tasks we take for granted. Consider wanting to roll over in bed, but finding you can't because the pain is way too intense. Many months later, tiny chores like putting on my underwear, being able to bend to sit on a toilet, drying my feet after showering or tying my shoelaces were beyond me. I needed assistance with everything, and still do with some of them. Luckily for me, I had (and have) the support of my extremely patient and wonderful family and friends to see me through this tough time. One benefit is that I get to enjoy regular pedicures!

For endless weeks, staring at the ceiling, I endured hours of not only physical, but emotional agony. Depressed, anxious, scared, guilty, doubtful, insecure – you name it. If there was any negative emotion to be had, I experienced it. Eventually I returned to work, doggedly getting through each day surviving on a cocktail of painkillers and endless treatments of physiotherapy, acupuncture and medical appointments, until eventually at 49 years of age and on a medical recommendation, I had to quit. What was I to do now that I no longer had a job? Should I simply feel sorry for myself? The answer to this burning question was an emphatic no!

My greatest learning was the moment I discovered my injury was not an obstacle. I couldn't let it defeat me, as I still had a long list of things I wanted to do before I departed this world. With the support of those closest to me, I couldn't leap over that obstacle, but I learned to crawl around it. I also discovered that with the emotional strength I knew I had deep inside me, I could believe it was possible to achieve those things I had dreamed of accomplishing as a little girl. I was not going to miss out on feeling, experiencing, being a part of and achieving the things I had forgotten or decided were not possible. It was simple. I had a choice: stagnate and shrivel, or pick myself up and move forward.

With the right kind of outlook, preparation and action, you can really make a difference in whether you are in control of your life, or sadly, a victim.

I chose not to be a victim! Instead, I founded www.fabat40.com, a wonderful community of the most fabulous women, with the aim to inspire, motivate and educate women beyond forty to empower themselves and their lives; to find, flaunt and fulfil the goddess that is in each and every one of us. And what an amazing journey I am now experiencing. I just love it, and cannot believe I am fortunate to now be able to live the life of my dreams, and at the same time enjoy and spread such passion.

Through the website, a community has been established and continues to grow, by meeting socially to share, network, become motivated and inspired by some of the best speakers, and enjoy learning about style, fashions, health and fitness, abundance and prosperity, and many topics which enable women to empower their lives.

One of the inevitabilities in life is ageing. No one has discovered the fountain of youth, or a cure to halt ageing, but you can minimize the negative effects of this process and turn the clock back by taking care of your mind, body and overall health. For many, midlife is clouded by fear, despair and disappointment that life has passed them by. Are you a person who dreads each birthday? Do you wonder what could have been? Do you hear yourself ask, "If only …?" Perhaps you had dreams and desires that are now locked away inside you with no hope of escaping and achieving.

The great news is that it's not too late! In fact, it's never too late to find true happiness and absolute fabulousness in your life. And my passion is to assist you on your journey of discovery and allow you to transform your life in the most amazing and powerful ways.

Begin by asking yourself a few questions.

- What do I want in life?
- What desires do I dare to dream?
- What is it that motivates and inspires me?
- What are the forces that are currently shaping my life?
- What areas in my life am I ignoring?
- What do I need to do to awaken my sexiness, style and pizzazz?
- How do I learn to sizzle?
- What do I need to do in order to live the life I love and become the goddess I desire to be?

Do you feel complete? Are you satisfied that you have achieved all you have ever wished for and that life couldn't be better? If that is so, congratulations and I wish you continued success in your future.

However, if you find that something is missing, whether in your relationships, wealth, health or career, my book series *Fabulous Beyond Forty*, will show you how to awaken, manifest and achieve the goddess inside you. These books have allowed me to achieve a dream that first emerged when I was a young girl of about 8 years of age. Being an avid reader, I had always wanted to write and now, my dream has been realized. The feeling of joy is indescribable as I succeed, and my desire now is to enable you too to awaken and achieve your own dreams; to experience the same feelings of joy and wholeness as I do.

And you can you know. You can live the life you love, be the goddess you desire to be and more importantly, the woman you deserve to be.

Be proud of who you are, what you have already experienced and achieved, and be grateful that you still have so much life ahead of you to finally spend as you desire. This book series provides tips, strategies and inspiration to educate, motivate and empower you as you live absolutely *Fabulous Beyond Forty*.

I am now living the life of my dreams. Are you?

I'd like to leave you with a wonderful thought by the late, great Audrey Hepburn, who looked fabulous at any age and stage of her life.

> *"People, more than things, have to be restored, renewed, revived, reclaimed and redeemed; never throw out anyone."*
> *Audrey Hepburn*

Being a wife and mother, **Danette** added Author, Speaker, NLP Master Practitioner, Wellness Coach, Motivational Mentor and founder of www.FabulousBeyondForty.com, all in her 49th year. She discovered that she had a choice in life – remain in her comfort zone, or follow her dreams. You can guess which path she chose and today her life is a celebration.

Visit www.FabulousBeyondForty.com to download your free bonuses including a 20 minute audio visualization to boost confidence and self-esteem.

BACK IN DADDY'S ARMS

Sharon Hill

"Daddy, you're my true love." Gracie spoke these precious words to her Daddy as he tucked her in and kissed her goodnight. My daughter, like most other four-year-old girls, loves fairytales, stories of princesses and princes falling in love and living happily ever after. Her Daddy is her 'prince', and her 'true love'. It warms my heart as I think about how different my little girl's experience is from my own.

My father was a violent alcoholic. His addiction not only destroyed his own life, it almost took the lives of those he cherished the most in the world.

I was the eldest of his five children – two daughters and three sons. His drunken, abusive rages confused the little girl that I once was. I knew he loved me, yet he could be so mean and cruel. It was a contradiction too hard for my young innocent mind to understand.

There were many happy times in my childhood, but sadly, the happiest were when my father was not at home. As a soldier in the Australian Army, he was often away. He spent extended periods of time overseas in Borneo and Vietnam. I missed my Daddy, but I didn't miss his abuse. Each time he returned, our home became the war zone again – and after his return from Vietnam, things only escalated.

I remember his masculine smell, the sweet, piquant fragrance of Old Spice, mixed with the warm tones of Californian Poppy, blended with subtle wafts of Brasso and boot polish, topped off crudely with the unmistakable reek of Bundaberg rum. But my most vivid memory is of the night that I lost my Daddy from my life.

I was eleven years old. My father had been drinking and an argument once again ensued between my parents. This time however it escalated to the point that my father became so enraged, he was intent on killing us all.

My mother hurried us all into the bedroom at the end of the hall and barricaded the door with furniture. She positioned herself, using her body as a wedge to prevent the door from being opened – to protect her little ones from the danger that threatened them on the other side.

We could hear him outside trying to get in, hacking at the door with a bayonet – the sounds of glass smashing and his terrifying threats to kill us all. Our fear was somewhat eased by our brave mother's soothing words, but after several hours, we could sense her strength waning. That's when terror truly set in.

When the police finally arrived, we all cried tears of relief. I felt safe in the policeman's strong arms as he carried me across the blanket of broken glass, but my heart had also been broken. I now felt safe, but at what price? My Daddy and I became separated from that day forward. We didn't even get to say goodbye. I was left with a void in my heart and a feeling of unworthiness that would haunt me for many years.

Within two years, my mother remarried and I had a new Daddy. He not only broke my heart, he deeply wounded my soul through the sexual abuse I suffered at his hands.

As time passed, I tried to put the past behind me, but the Daddy-shaped space in my heart cried out to be filled. So many times I craved for my father's love, but it was nowhere to be found.

My life became a journey of trying unsuccessfully to fill the empty space in my heart and becoming more wounded in the process. I found myself in unhealthy and abusive relationships, and even questioning my own dismal existence during a two-year battle with chronic depression – until I finally turned to God and true healing began to take place. In God, I found myself back in my Daddy's arms.

But this is not the end of the story. Just last year I received a phone call that would change my life forever. At the time I was working on my book which I had decided to title *Back in Daddy's Arms* – an autobiographical book focusing on my loss of my Daddy and my discovery of the love of my Heavenly Father. At that stage, I had no idea of just how much more there was to the title of my book – and my story.

My father was in a nursing home with only weeks to live. After over thirty years, God gave me the opportunity to be reunited with my Daddy.

As hard as it was to visit him, I knew in my heart that I must. I had been going through a real transformation in my own life and I believed that my father deserved a chance to heal his own wounded heart.

Memories flashed through my mind; I saw him grab my three-year-old brother by the hair and hurl him violently against the wall; I heard his vicious, hateful words, his threats...my little brother's cries... my mother's desperate screams...her comforting words to her precious little ones, through her silent, desperate sobs of despair...

Yes, he had made some mistakes, but so had I. He had already missed out on so much – watching his five children grow up and have families of their own; being a grandfather to his thirteen grandchildren. He did not deserve to die a lonely old man.

I visited him in the hope that it would bring some joy into the last days of his life, but I didn't anticipate just how much these visits would do for me – for that little girl inside me who had just wanted her Daddy's love, her Daddy's hugs and kisses – that special love that only a Daddy can give.

He was a grumpy, frail old man. He looked much older than he was, certainly much older than I remembered him, but my heart recognized him. I remember looking at his bony, nicotine-stained hands and thinking how they were once the chubby young hands of a little boy trying to tie his shoelaces and write his name for the very first time. They were the same hands that had caressed his beautiful young wife and held me, his first born baby daughter, but they were also the hands that had caused so much pain to those he loved.

Yet the man I saw that day was no threat to anyone anymore. In fact, he gave me the most special gift. I was given the opportunity to tell him I loved him and forgave him for not being there for me.

I shared with him about what God had done in my life, how much God loved him and wanted to forgive him. My father was convinced that he would spend eternity in hell, but I was with him when he made his peace with God and the weight of his self-condemnation was lifted from his heart. And this time, we got to say goodbye.

"I love you too," he said as we hugged. It was the first time I remember him ever saying those precious words to me – and as he spoke them I realized that I was back in my Daddy's arms.

Sharon is an inspirational Speaker, Success Coach and Author of *Back in Daddy's Arms – an inspirational true story of lives transformed through love and forgiveness.* She is passionate about seeing women freed from the bondage of shame, negative self-image and self-constructed walls of protection that prevent them from becoming the inspirational people they were truly meant to be.

For a free chapter of Sharon's book go to
www.BackinDaddysArms.com/freechapter.html
on her website at www.BackinDaddysArms.com or email her at
sharon@BackinDaddysArms.com.

ACCESS SUCCESS:

CREATING THE POSITIVE CORE MINDSET WITHIN YOURSELF

Mark Victor Hansen

Before you can live a prosperous life, a state of well-being where you flourish and thrive, you have to create a positive core mindset, or belief system, within yourself. Why? It isn't possible to live a healthy, positive life without a healthy, positive mindset from which you base your life. You see, everything that is drawn to you in the physical world is a result of what is going on inside of your mental world.

You are where you are because your thinking made it so

Where you are in your life, at this every moment, is because of your core belief system, your mindset. Your beliefs, what you really believe deep down inside, have created whatever success or failures you have had. Most of the time there is no one else to blame. What you have experienced throughout your life has been produced directly from beliefs of lack, low self-esteem and limitation. You have created your life with your beliefs. If you want to change it – change your belief system.

Although many people base their current financial or emotional situations on the belief that there is a shortage of this or a limited number of that – they are lying to themselves. The truth is that there is no lack or shortage. These beliefs are only in the mind. We have imposed them on ourselves, but they are not real.

You owe it to yourself to think only unlimited prosperity

It is a belief that has to begin with you, because your personal wealth and abundance begins and ends within your mind. You are in control of it. What we believe becomes our reality. What we concentrate our conscious minds upon is returned to us. We need to go way beyond the way we normally think and into the world of phenomenal success and wondrous possibilities. My audio program **How to Think Bigger Than You Ever Thought You Could Think** can help you do just that.

My friend, the late great Norman Vincent Peale, said that he was born with an inferiority complex. When he wrote the book **The Power of Positive Thinking** he was rejected by every publisher he approached. Dr. Peale came home one day feeling disheartened and at the end of his rope. Dr. Peale threw this manuscript for his book into the trash and told his wife, Ruth not to take it out. Dr. Peale felt that he was a horrible writer and a complete failure.

His wife, Ruth knew better. She did not take the book out of the trashcan. Rather, she took the book in the trashcan to a publisher who read it and said that the book was amazing. The publisher published the book. That book is an American classic and just had its 50th anniversary. It is one of the most successful self-help books ever written.

Luckily, Ruth believed in her husband and his book enough for success to take root. Our beliefs in, or against, something pre-determines the outcome of any situation we encounter. Believe you are abundantly wealthy and you will be. Believe that you are a disastrous failure... and you will be. The choice is yours.

The secret to success – overcoming fear

The secret to being successful and having abundance lies within all of us. In order to have everything we want we must become conscious thinkers and speakers. Why think and speak consciously? Because the words have power – once thought or spoken, they take on a life of their own and set the Universe in motion. Words and thoughts are amazing entities. Negative thoughts and worlds will defeat the most brilliant person, and usually, they are the result of one thing – fear.

In my audio program and book, **The Aladdin Factor**, I discuss the fact that there is only one true enemy – and that is fear. Fear is the enemy that destroys dreams and crushes possibilities. It is the reason so many people never realize their greatest desires. How does one overcome fear? There is only one way – feel the fear and do it anyway. Fear will always be there. The difference between the greatest achievers and those who have never succeeded lies in one thing – they both felt the fear, but the greatest achievers pushed through their fear and did what they had to do. But you can transform fear into courage by charging through it. Action eradicates fear. No matter what you fear, positive, self-affirming action can diminish or completely cancel that which you are fearful of.

Adjust your attitude

The world in which you live is determined by your attitude. It is the thing that will make or break you, because it is your attitude that helps to determine your belief system. Negative attitude – negative thoughts – negative belief system – negative results. Positive attitude – positive thoughts – positive belief system – positive results.

Where did all this negativity come from to begin with?

It all begins with just one negative thought. Then, like a snowball rolling down a snow covered hill, it gathers mass and momentum. Pretty soon the negative thoughts grown bigger and bigger until you are consumed by them. They become the only thoughts you can think. Someone mentions a phenomenal opportunity that could be great for your family or career and you immediately shut them down – you won't even attempt to try because negativity has destroyed the idea of possibility from your mind.

First, think exclusively of prosperity & positivity

The first step to changing your core mindset is to take a look at your present belief system.

Do you believe that you have no control over what happens to you? Is fate in control of your destiny? Do you think that events happen randomly in life and success is just the luck of the draw? Are you overwhelmed by the thought that you could have even the smallest influence over your own success or failure?

What do you believe about yourself?

Do you believe you are worthy of abundance? Do you think that somehow other people are more deserving of success that you are? Do you believe that there is a shortage of supply and that there is only enough wealth and prosperity for a select percentage of the population?

Your beliefs about the world and yourself are what you should concentrate on. These beliefs are the most important because they are the lenses through which you see everyone and everything.

No matter what your current situation is, no matter how bad you think you have it, I want you to understand something. You have, at your very fingertips, the ability to tap the wealth of the Universe. All you have to do is believe. Change your core belief system and you change your life. It's true! All you have to do is believe.

Whatever you concentrate on, whether it's positive or negative, will manifest itself into physical form right before your eyes

After you have examined you belief system, it is time to mold it to fit your idea of an abundant life. How do you begin to do this? By thinking exclusively of success and prosperity. If you are not as successful as you'd like to be it is because you have allowed negative thoughts to run in your brain like a movie reel. This must be stopped. I'm not saying that negative thoughts won't *try* to enter your head. They will. You must learn to stop them and immediately replace them with positive thoughts. Keep changing the VHS in your head, until you see what you've been releasing in your mind's eye. My friend Jim Rohn says: *"Don't start a day until you've finished it. Don't start a week until you've finished it. Don't start a year until you've finished."* Meaning, visualize positively from the end result and your results will vastly improve now.

We must first believe it before we can achieve it

We are in control of our thinking. Only we can determine what we will think about. It's just as easy to think positive thoughts, as it is to think of negative thoughts. So, why not concentrate on the positive and have amazing results? In order to have everything we want in our lives we need to discipline our minds to think solely of prosperity. We must stop negative thinking as soon as it begins, because negative thoughts do not hold any hope for success in them. Think only of abundance and you will attract abundance. Thinking of poverty and despair will only make you poor and desperate.

Whatever you concentrate on, whether it's positive or negative, will manifest itself into physical form right before your eyes.

Mark Victor Hansen is the co-creator of the wildly successful Chicken Soup for the Soul® series, and the co-author of a new book, *The One Minute Millionaire*. For more than 25 years he has influenced society's top leaders, and the general public, on a global scale, speaking over 50 times a year. He is also an active entrepreneur, philanthropist and humanitarian. Mark Victor Hansen is an enthusiastic crusader of what's possible and is driven to make the world a better place. For more information please visit www.MarkVictorHansen.com.

POWERFUL SECRETS:

A LIFE-CHANGING JOURNEY OF DISCOVERY

Cecilia Nannini

An Open Mind

My first experience of talking to a clairvoyant blew me away. I didn't know if I believed in it or not, but I was curious. As a publisher and editor of a lifestyle magazine I had the perfect excuse to go see one. I decided to do an issue on "Clairvoyance, spirituality and alternative medicine."

How convenient! I could disguise my curiosity and fascination as "research" and people would not look at me as if I was a bit strange. After all, I had studied science at university level and I had a business degree, both very "serious" fields of study.

The one thing the visit to the clairvoyant did for me was shatter some life-long concepts I held that determined how I viewed the world. Any doubts I may have had about clairvoyants being able to 'see' the future was completely eliminated. She told me in great detail about the present, as well as things that were to happen to me 3 years in the future. I realized that my view of the world and my idea of time had to be completely re-evaluated. How could anyone see things that did not yet exist?

At this point one thing became clear to me: I needed to approach life with an open mind. There was more out there than I knew about. There were things I needed to find out - about life, the universe and me.

My Life Hits Rock Bottom

Shortly after the visit with the clairvoyant, my life hit rock bottom. I was, at the time, in my late thirties, and lived in a modest but comfortable home in a well-to-do suburb with my partner. I had started a magazine publishing business so that I could work from home. My intention was to start a family. However, my partner, being four years younger than me, was not keen on the idea. He didn't want the extra stress of supporting a child and me. I knew I would need to prove that I could still earn an income and look after our child, as having my children looked after by someone else was not for me.

The solution therefore, was to have my own business I could run from home, have flexible hours, and look after the children at the same time. Sounded perfect! NOT!

Within two years, not only did I not have a child, I didn't have a partner, a house, a job or any assets. I had lost everything. I had invested all my net worth into the publication. My partner had bought my share of the value of our house so I could invest the money into the magazine. The tension and stress of the business was causing problems in my relationship and after 12 years together, we separated. I had to move out of my home.

Although I had achieved break-even point on the sixth issue of the magazine, there was nothing left for working capital to keep the operation going. I was feeling like I was pushing a very heavy wheelbarrow up a very steep hill. I had tried everything I could think of, but it just wasn't working. I should have been able to do this. Where was I going wrong? I had to admit I had failed.

Dark Night Of The Soul

It was the worst time of my life. I felt exhausted and feeling a huge loss. I felt alone and very scared. I still owed creditors about $25,000. I woke up in the middle of the night feeling as if I was at the bottom of a deep, dark well. I was so far down I couldn't see any light above or how to get out. I was crying. I even briefly considered suicide as one of my options, but I just could not have caused that sort of grief to my parents. I felt hopeless. I surrendered. This was my 'dark night of the soul.'

44

That night something happened. I woke up a different person. Things started to fall into place. Opportunities started to present themselves. A friend told me of a great job that seemed tailor-made for me. Having seized that opportunity, I negotiated with the banks for a loan to pay off the creditors. Information I needed seemed to come to me just when I needed it. Oprah was doing the *Remembering Your Spirit* series and was having great, inspiring guests on her show. I would follow up leads, buy books, and read everything I could. I was fascinated, amazed, and inspired. I did courses in meditation. I was waking up little by little to an awesome world.

I had started my journey of discovery.

The Journey of Discovery

Along this journey, I discovered *Powerful Secrets*: the Law of Attraction, the power of now. I learned to distinguish between my ego and my true self, the observer, and how to choose what was right for me. I learned how to listen and trust my emotional guidance system. I learned to accept that everything is as it should be, and found out about my life's nine-year cycles and how to work with these to empower my life. I discovered how to ask the Universe for what I needed and remain patient while I waited for it to deliver. I learned to recognize when the deliveries came in, and take the appropriate action in order to receive them. And most importantly, I learned to be grateful for everything that was coming into my life.

I now know whatever we are experiencing in our lives, whether wanted or unwanted, we are responsible for. I realize each of us has the power, if not the know-how, to attract what we want to experience in our lives. This to me is AMAZING. Why are we not all living this way?

I decided my purpose in life was to help as many people as I could with this life-changing wisdom, so they too can live the life they desire.

My Passion

I now spend my life doing what I am passionate about, passing on all the secrets and techniques that have helped me. Through tele-seminars, my writing and my newsletter, I share everything that has worked for me: what steps you need to take; why it works and why it sometimes doesn't; and how you can improve your skills to make it work every time. Whatever area of your life you want to improve - financial, career, relationship, weight, health, parenting - this wisdom and know-how can be applied. On my website _www.PowerfulSecretS. com_ I offer free resources on how to start turning your life around.

I now have the life I have always wanted. In a period of five short years I have gone from having nothing to owning a lovely home in a great location. I work from a glass-front studio at the back of my house, overlooking a leafy garden and a lily pond, with my golden retriever dog lying under my desk.

I make a living doing what I love and what I'm passionate about. And yes, my life allows me the flexibility to stay at home and look after my wonderful daughter. For me, life doesn't get much better than this.

And if I can do it, you can too!

Cecilia Nannini is a personal empowerment mentor, life coach, author and mother of a beautiful daughter. Her love and passion is to inspire and empower others to create the life they want for themselves. Her approach is to share the powerful secrets and techniques that have made such an impact in her life. Visit her website, www.PowerfulSecretS.com for a FREE Special Report - _Top 10 Most Powerful Secrets to Empower Your Life._

Finding My One True Love

Sharon E. Donnelly

Once Upon a Time

My childhood was filled with movies showing me that women were damsels in distress and needed their very own Prince Charming to whisk them away from their troubles. Only then would they find true happiness. I remember being a young girl and dreamily humming to myself one of songs from the movie Snow White, "Some day my prince will come." At five years old I fantasized that one day I would meet my very own handsome prince. He would rescue me and we would live happily ever after. It took me years to shake off this notion of needing a prince and a fairy tale romance.

Mirror, Mirror on the Wall - Who is the Fairest of Them All?

When we start out in the world, we view everything with wonder. Everything is new and special and we are complete just as we are. It doesn't take long before we are taught to look outside ourselves to surface details and the destructive fantasy cycle begins.

Little by little we get conditioned to look on the outside for happiness. Distractions begin to emerge in the form of television, advertisements, magazines, and other people that will tell us that we need more or that we are not enough as we are. This will cause us to doubt our attractiveness, intelligence, and ability to be accepted in this world. That is where the confusion begins.

One vivid scene in the movie Snow White, depicted a wicked Queen looking into a mirror and asking, "Mirror, mirror on the wall, who is the fairest of them all?" The mirror would answer back and the Queen would be happy or enraged based upon the mirror's words.

It's easy to look outside ourselves to measure our worth. People spend their entire lives looking for true love outside themselves. They try to fix themselves in an external way to appeal to whatever they are attracted to, their mate or so-called love, not realizing that they have their true love with them their entire lives. Your true love has been inside you from the day you were born. That person is you.

Letting Go of Living With Illusions: Giving Up the Fantasy

How do you escape this fantasy world? You must look within. Inside of you exists a never-ending pool of inner-strength, answers to life's complexities and personal acceptance. Avoiding or ignoring your own inner-voice is a way of life for most people and that always gets them into trouble. Your worth is not determined by how much you weigh, how much money you have, or what kind of car you drive. In fact, it does not come from the outside at all - it comes from within. It comes from self love. This is simply your natural state of being connected to yourself.

One of the first steps in finding happiness and loving yourself is to give up the concern of what other people might think of you. You have all you need and are beautiful and loveable just as you are. If you don't believe that, then you are caught up in the illusions that keep you stuck. Once you begin to look for happiness and acceptance from the outside, you are setting yourself up for temporary fixes that never truly stick.

Fall in Love With Yourself

Falling in love with yourself can be one of the most difficult yet exhilarating changes you will experience. It begins by cultivating a relationship with yourself and will require intense personal exploration. It also comes from allowing yourself to being fully present in each moment. It means checking in with yourself to identify your wants, needs, aspirations, purpose, and what ignites your passion.

People often resist who they are and what their needs may be, and if anything, punish themselves. Be aware of making negative statements to yourself. Acknowledge the fearful side from which these thoughts came and replace these thoughts with more positive ones. It is like being a loving parent to oneself.

You don't have to do this exploration alone. As a counselor, I am grateful for the experience of working with people on their journey of falling in love with who they are.

Cinderella: A Victim or Victor?

Cinderella was perfectly content with her life before she lost her father. When he died, she was put in a situation where she was bullied by her stepmother and step-sisters. Life will throw curve balls at us. Often painful and seemingly tragic, they can be viewed as either gifts or opportunities. Will you accept these gifts presented before you? It is your choice on what you do with them. You are not a victim unless you chose to be one. You can develop new strengths, personal growth, and wisdom as you take action toward developing an empowered life.

You can gain excitement, even when something fails, because it means you have learned something new. History is filled with the stories of women whose greatness was achieved primarily through the resilience with which they met and overcame adversities. Are you still waiting for your Prince Charming to arrive or can you become your own personal hero and rescue yourself?

You have to take responsibility for your own life. If you don't like things, change what you can. Being a victim is boring and it annoys other people. If you find your life is out of harmony, you need to take action to change it. Otherwise circumstances will take care of themselves and you will feel powerless. When you take responsibility for your life, you gain self-esteem and start living an authentic life. You are true to yourself and everything in your world will feel right.

Modern Day Bullies: Obstacles to Finding Your True Love

Once you break out of this fantasy trap and begin your journey towards finding your true love, you will be confronted with modern-day villains. They are fear, doubt, shame, living in the past, and not accepting your complete self. Be brave. The moment you release yourself from these saboteurs, your energy will change and will ripple into all areas of your life. You will realize all of the things that matter are right in front of you. They include creativity, joy, and inner-peace.

Your Own Glass Slipper

It is true that love can rescue you and bring you a lifetime of happiness, but this love has to come from the self first. Other people and relationships help to bring out with is already within us. The more you are filled with love for yourself, the more you will have to give to others. Conversely, if you don't have self-love, no amount of love outside of yourself can sustain you.

In this world, you have to be a complete and whole person first and not look for wholeness outside of yourself. You need to walk your journey with your own inner-strength and completeness and stand on your own two feet, glass slippers and all. No prince can do that for you.

Breaking out of the fairytale and finding your own true love within yourself is an exciting journey of reflection and self-care. Once we return to the basics, we can reclaim that bliss for life that was natural to us as children.

You too can say, *"And I lived happily ever after!"*

Sharon Donnelly, M.S., LCADC, HHC, founder of **True to Self Health** is an advocate for health and wellness as a licensed clinician, certified health counselor, professor, and international author. Sharon helps people see the connection between the food they eat, thoughts they think, and its powerful effect on their health, energy, mood, and ability to have a more authentic and empowered life. To receive her FREE newsletter visit her website at www.TrueToSelfHealth.com or email her at TrueToSelfHealth@gmail.com.

Sacked to Successful

Charyn Youngson

Turning 40 was a milestone in more ways than one for me. Someone asked me shortly before I turned 40 if I was happy with my life so far and did I have any regrets. I mentally started reassessing my life and came to the conclusion that I had not been happy for a very long time and the only one who could change that situation was me. So I decided to end my unhappy marriage, stand on my own two feet and take a bold step to reclaim my happiness.

Suddenly I became a single Mum of two teenagers still attending high school, and was working as an Administration Assistant in a nursing home earning a fairly low income. Working with the elderly was a pure delight and every day I woke up happy to go off to work. I had a great boss who appreciated the extra effort and we were a great team. Then due to ill health my boss left work, in came the new boss and my bubble was somewhat burst.

It didn't happen overnight, but my new boss and I just didn't really click. No matter how hard I worked, nothing ever seemed good enough for the new boss. Our relationship deteriorated to the point where her behaviour towards me started to undermine my confidence and affect my health. It became a struggle to go to work and put on a happy face. Eventually I had enough and I made a formal complaint of bullying against my boss. The company management initially supported me and organized mediation between the two of us. During the mediation time I moved to another work location until the 6 weeks that it took to finish the process had ended. After the mediation was complete, I was allowed back to my work site and I felt confident that the bad feelings had been resolved.

A couple of weeks after returning to work, I went on 2 weeks holiday. When I returned to work, I found my office cleaned out and my boss nowhere to be seen. I was about to go searching for her when I was confronted by a senior manager in the organization who presented me with a letter saying I had to attend a meeting the next day to discuss my future with the company. She then asked me to go home and escorted me off the premises like I was a criminal. I returned the next day to be told I was sacked and see you later! To say I was devastated was an understatement. I was now an unemployed single mother relying on benefits until I found another job.

Luckily I have always been a positive person, and have always believed that when one door closes, another one opens. That opening door was joining Wildly Wealthy Women, a women's mentoring program whose philosophy is to teach women how to create wealth and abundance using practical tools, knowledge and a Millionaire Mindset. I set off for Queensland to attend my first Wildly Wealthy Weekend and was dumbstruck to find myself surrounded by over 500 other like minded women from all over Australia.

At the end of that inspiring weekend, I returned home with a totally new mindset and a new career path firmly planted in my psyche. Real estate had always interested me and I felt I now had the knowledge to be able to create wealth though property investing. I was determined to start creating wealth and achieve financial freedom through buying and renovating houses. I was going to be a property investor! The day I changed my thoughts was the day I changed my life.

One of Sandy Forster's motivating sayings from that weekend stuck in my mind - *"Fake it until you make it."* The first thing I did was order business cards that said Charyn Youngson – Property Investor. I started attending open house inspections introducing myself to the real estate agents as a Property Investor, letting them know that I was looking for 'renovator's delight' properties, and generally portraying myself as already quite experienced.

I refinanced my home, set up my company, and scoured the real estate pages and internet for suitable 'fix it uppers.' Within two weeks I found a property that was exactly what I was looking for –

a Foreclosure Sale. I went and examined the house carefully, took photos, mentally planned what needed to be done to it and did all the due diligence that was required. It would be the perfect house to renovate, **if** I could purchase it. In a conversation with my accountant Martienne I mentioned the property that I had seen. I told her that I had never been to an auction before, so the likelihood of me getting the house was pretty slim. Martienne said, "Charyn, yes you can get it…if you believe in yourself!" I put the photo of the house on my computer as my screen saver, and looked at it every day leading up to the auction imagining that the house was already mine!

On a warm, sunny Saturday morning I nervously waited with a handful of other possible buyers for the auction to begin. No one else was bidding, so I stuck my hand up before the auctioneer was about to pass the house in. This prompted someone else to bid, then my hand went up again, and on went the process until all of a sudden the house was mine! I had purchased a derelict house for $109,000. I was on my way.

Walking back into that house on settlement day I thought, "What have I done? Where I am I going to start? This place is a disaster!" but I quickly put those thoughts aside and just started. I had a plan and a budget. Paint trays and rollers became my new best friends. I painted the entire interior of the house and even the exterior walls as well. I installed new carpets, took measurements for a new kitchen, and with the help of a friend, totally transformed the derelict house into a showpiece in four weeks. With borrowed pieces of furniture to make it look like a home, I put it on the market and it sold within a month. The renovations cost $12,000 and for the selling price was $156,000. I made about $30,000 which was more than I had earned in a whole year working as an Admin Assistant!

I was now definitely a Property Investor! No going back to working for a boss or having to rely on anyone else to support me.

In three years I have gone on to triple my income from buying, renovating and selling houses. I became an expert in fast, inexpensive makeovers and decided to start my own consultancy business advising clients on how to achieve the maximum sale price for their homes using my DIY techniques.

I love to share my knowledge and it is part of my philosophy to inspire other people. For the past year I have been teaching a class with the Workers Education Australia (WEA) called "Renovating for Profit." I am also writing a book about renovating and makeover tips and hope to inspire a larger range of people to get out there and do it themselves!

I am now living the life I dreamed about 3 years ago and I continue to revise my vision for the future. Dream it, believe it and those dreams will become reality. For if I can do it, anyone can.

Charyn Youngson, Director of *Houses to Impress,* specialises in assisting clients to increase the value in their homes. She gives them ideas using easy, inexpensive DIY techniques to create a WOW factor that helps them to achieve the best possible price. Charyn likes to inspire other people to renovate for profit and is currently writing a book on her renovating experiences. Find some makeover inspiration at her website www.HousesToImpress.com or contact her at HousesToImpress@optusnet.com

WHY IS CHANGE SO HARD?

Debbie Thomas

You want to change something about yourself, your life, your weight, your relationships, maybe even your business. You really, really, really want to change. You've tried everything you can think of and still, here you are. *Why* is it so hard? No matter what you try, nothing changes.

Well, I'm sure you've heard the saying that we only use less than 10% of our brain capacity, right? That's true in one respect - only about 10% of our brain is involved with our consciousness, what we actually think about and dream about and consciously do. The other 90% is our subconscious brain function. This 90% is making sure we breathe, pump blood, grow hair, sweat to cool off and produce saliva to swallow. It's making sure that every single microscopic cell in our bodies gets the oxygen and nutrients it needs, then removes the waste products from those cells and sends them to our inner trash can - 24/7. When we want to grab something, we don't consciously think "lift arm, open fingers, move 3.67895 inches forward, 1.96875432 inches to the left, close fingers".... you get the drift. No, our conscious mind just thinks "I want to grab that" and this 90% of our brain fires off a message in a fraction of a second, to millions of nerve endings that make your body move to the exact coordinates that you want it to move to and grab that thing. Your conscious mind has little or no clue about the zillions of tasks that it is performing every single milisecond.

This **sub**-conscious part of your mind knows the routine. It's got it all down to a science. It's learned everything it needs to know and exactly what it takes to make you, well, **you**, and it is as set in its ways as anything you can imagine. It is perfectly happy with you the way you are and sees no need to readjust anything.

This 90% of your mind is extremely powerful. It will resist your conscious desire to change by doing any number of things including:

- Ignoring you – "Who needs this personal development stuff? Big deal. Besides, it's kind of touchy feely and that's for fruitcakes."

- Contradicting you – You affirm "I am a millionaire" and your subconscious "Belief Detective" responds with "Yeah, right! Have you **looked** at your bank balance lately?"

- Making you doubt yourself – "I don't need to change. If I did change, who would I be? If I didn't have this fear, or this anger, or this (fill in the blank), I wouldn't be *me* anymore – right? People might notice."

- Procrastination – "This is too boring. I'm tired. Just a few more games of solitaire, then I'll get around to reading this silly book."

- Sabotage – "Forget it. I'll never be good enough, or smart enough, or pretty enough or (again, fill in the blank) enough to be successful, so why even try? That's for special people, not me."

I know this because I said these very things to myself for decades. So you see, *you* may want to change – but *it* doesn't. That's a problem since *it* controls you - down to each and every atom that makes up every molecule, every cell of your body. *It* has the distinct advantage in this tug of war. *It* is designed by the universe to take care of you and that's what *it* thinks *it* is doing.

Think of your subconscious mind like the waters of a river flowing downstream. A farmer (your conscious mind) suddenly decides that he wants the river to change its course to flow closer to his fields so he can use it to irrigate them. That river is going to keep right on flowing the way it always has, and doesn't care a fig for the farmer's wishes. He can demand that the river flow his way; he can ask and plead and pitch a royal tizzy for the river to change – the river doesn't even pay attention. He can even start to dig an irrigation channel, but the river keeps right on going for the most part. It may notice the channel being dug, but will ignore it or attempt to wash it out so it can pass right on by. The farmer is going to have to convince the river to come his way. He is going to have to teach the river by digging that channel all the way to his fields in order to change the flow of things. He's going to have to show the river that it is easier for the river to come to him, than it is for the river to follow the path it's always known. **That** will take work and that's why it's so hard to change. It takes dedication, focus, patience and **work**.

You have to do the same kind of work to train your subconscious mind to make the changes you desire. You have to keep on repeating the things you want to change. You have to convince your subconscious "Belief Detective" that what you want is what *is.* You have to work to build up new neural networks in your brain until your subconscious mind finally agrees and thinks "Okay; this is the way things are going to be from now on." It will then, and only then, take over the everyday tasks necessary to make this new you thrive. It is mental work instead of physical work, but it still takes dedication, focus, patience and **work**. The only way to make the work easier is to trick your subconscious by making the work feel like fun! That's where AttitudeZapz! Affirmation Jingles come in.

You've got to keep connecting those networks and shoring up that channel until it is fully done and the flow is absolute - and that means repetition. You've got to keep going, even when it rains and washes some of your work away. That means you can't sit there and feel sorry for yourself because you've had a setback. You have to bounce right back and start digging again. AttitudeZapz! can help you either way. As you are digging along, you've got this little song in your head telling you to keep on going...

"When I believe it I will see it,
It has to come to be.

When I believe it I will see this,
Or something better come to me."

And when the bad days come, as they surely will, you've got a secret weapon to blast through that "poor me" attitude. You've got a little song to reach for that tells you that no matter what...

"I've got an attitude of gratitude,
Yeah, that's my style.
Whatever comes to me,
I'm thankful all the while."

That's your work. These AttitudeZapz! are the repetition and the tool to bounce back, all in one. They are just little songs that you get stuck in your head. It's as simple as that. **Change really is possible** when you know how and you've got the right tools to make it fun.

Debbie is a living testament to the notion that change is possible. She always wanted to do something to help others while helping herself, but tried and failed miserably countless times. Now in her mid fifties she has found her passion. Her life has totally changed and she now lives every day making her vision bright for all who need help finding their own destiny. To learn more and get a FREE AttitudeZapz!, visit www.AttitudeZapz.com.

THE JOURNEY TO FIND MY DESIRE

Hidemi Chida

Sometimes in life, things don't happen the way we plan.
My husband and daughters had gone out shopping one Sunday afternoon, while I was having coffee on the veranda in the backyard. I was feeling rather empty inside as my daughters were soon going to be moving out from our home.

I then realized that if my husband and I were both to retire, we would live out our remaining days one slow, quietly passing day after another. At that moment, I started to wonder, "What sort of life could I have that would be satisfying and fun, plus allow me to stay active after we retire?"

Unexpectedly, my husband's job became redundant, and the choices for new employment were limited. I'm Japanese and had always been a good cook, so we opened a small Japanese restaurant. It was very exciting at the beginning, yet we didn't have a business plan and not much business experience to draw from. Five years later, our business had failed. We had gone from being debt free to owing $100,000. Because of that, I lost all my confidence, and I didn't know what to do next. I was now in my 50's and I decided this was really a good chance to find my true desire in life, rather than jumping into just any job for money.

While I was searching for my true desire, I read books to help. Suddenly one day the thought "I want to travel Europe as a backpacker" popped into my head. That was my forgotten dream. "No way! I can't do this!" was my response, so I pushed the idea away. I would feel guilty for leaving my husband and daughters and travelling alone for 3 months. I knew I was not happy with my life which had been turned upside down, but I decided to go even though we had large debts and I have a bad back. I was also worried about travelling alone at my age. To get the money to go, I sold my car and borrowed from the bank. My 20 year old daughter wanted to come along with me and we both wanted to find our true desire. I gave permission to myself to take a break from life.

While I enjoyed travelling, I thought, "I haven't found my desire from it."

After I returned home, life went along as usual. I didn't tell others the whole story of my valuable experiences through my travels. I wanted to write a book to share these stories, but I couldn't write in English. I published a book in Japanese, and named it "*Backpacker Mama*" by Hidemi Adams. I was exhausted by the whole writing and publishing process which took 2 years. While I was writing the book, I had gone to college to learn English and computer courses for a year. Once I could read English books, I felt I had discovered another world, the door to which for a long time had been closed to me. Wow!

When my daughters moved out of our house, my husband and I wanted to live different lifestyles and we finally separated. So I started a new life in Queensland at the age of 55. I lived in my own apartment, had free time and could use my money for whatever I liked. I was happy! Then suddenly I was hit by a depression from living in an unknown place with no family, friends or job and being totally alone. I couldn't find meaning to my life. I didn't want to do anything. I didn't even mind the thought of dying. I stayed inside my apartment, watching people passing by, and the television became my companion. I couldn't blame anyone for my life but me and I was the only one who could get me out from under the depression.

I remember reading a Robert Kiyosaki book. From that point on, I wanted to become a property investor, as I realized it would give me financial freedom – one of the reasons for my depression. I started to study, read books and listen to motivational CD's every day. Every word was new to me, and even though I suffered from headaches and backaches, I felt I wasn't going anywhere with my endless studying.

However, six months later, I started to look around for houses to buy, as by then I understood the theory behind property investment. I bought my first investment property, sold my apartment and bought land. I understood that even if I didn't know all the in's and out's of being an investor, it was still possible to succeed.

I realized there are different ways to gain a secure income. I attended a motivational seminar for the first time. I concentrated on studying the information and reading books which I got from the seminars. While I was studying I kept a diary. It was the only place I could express my true feelings. I ended up spending 2-4 hours writing in it each day. I even forgot to tidy up the house. I thought, "I must like to write", as this was something that no-one could take away from me. "If I can live like this, I'll be so happy," I thought. That's the point when I accepted my intuitive message.

But the door had not opened for me when I mingled with English speaking people. When I attended a writer's workshop, I was the only person there who was struggling to speak English. On one occasion we were just playing a game where everyone had to say a few sentences. I couldn't say what I wanted to say. I felt dumb!

When I got home from the writer's workshop, I hit a wall and punched a pillow in sheer anger and frustration. I stood in front of the mirror and said to myself, "What do you want?" "I want to express how I feel in writing", came the reply. "Is that what you really want?" "Yes, that's what I want. At this moment, I don't need a nice house, furniture or car", was the answer. "Then why don't you move towards that goal?" After saying these words I realized, "Yes, I found my desire."

After all those hungry and desperate situations, I finally found my true desire. It had taken me 5 years. I decided to become a writer so I can express how I feel about life, people, and cultures, and also I want to send a message to the next generation.

When we find our true desire, we find any obstacles in our path can easily be overcome by raising our spiritual power. By finding your true desire, your life can have unlimited happiness, and it will be easier to live in the moment and for your future.

Go for it!

Hidemi Chida is managing director and founder of "Active 50 Plus Women." She has lived in Japan and Australia and knows both country's lifestyle and culture. Her experience as a teacher, cook, dressmaker, Bonsai artist, business owner, traveler, and author has given her a unique perspective on life after 50. She has a passion to find real joy in retired life.

Visit www.Active50PlusWomen.com to get FREE "10 tips to Find Your True Desire."

DARE TO DREAM BIG AND
ONLY SETTLE FOR THE BEST

Sonja Bendz

Sitting on a big terrace with many colourful flowers, I am enjoying the beautiful view over the ocean. Down on the beach I hear the voices of my daughter and other children playing in the water and jumping trough the waves. Their voices are full of happiness, enjoyment and excitement.

Feeling deep gratitude I remind myself of how lucky we are for all the blessings that we have. Just a year ago our lives were totally different.

We were homeless. I had lost my home, my business, a luxury life stile... and most of my friends and family, too! I had no idea where my life was going or what I could possibly do next. Desperately I was asking myself how I would start from zero with no money, no high education, no special skills, in a new country with no friends and family, and a small child to take care of. I was powerless, filled with fear, worry and panic for our future.

It was hard for me to forget the past and accept the reality. Over and over I was dwelling, analyzing, thinking, and talking about my bad luck, regrets, mistakes, challenges, and my dramas, which only attracted more and more of them into my life. Going deeper and deeper down, I finally decided to let go of the past and move on! I relieved all my bad memories and let them go.

I remembered how I changed after that. I felt wonderfully alive, light, and peaceful with a deep sense of gratitude for all I already had: my precious daughter, health and a whole life in front of us. I felt gratitude and forgiveness to all involved in my life, for without them

I wouldn't be me. They made me learn, grow, and become this great unique person.

I reminded myself of the day when we first arrived here. It was a beautiful, sunny day. Walking on a street lined with palm trees and colourful flowers on either side, I was enjoying the precious view of the ocean and listening to the crashing of the waves. It was a magical place where you deeply felt the power of the ocean. Standing on the beach and looking at the horizon, I felt "at one" with the Universe, filled with magical calmness and total resignation to the moment. I had never before felt this way. I fell in love with this special place.

Nearby, there were beautiful apartments with big terraces facing the ocean. "Ah, what a paradise it could be to live there," I thought.

Deep in my soul I felt a deep, strong, burning desire to live here.

My 9 year old daughter was next to me and looking at the same place. Her eyes were full of nostalgia, love and expectation. My whole body started gently to shake from love, desire and courage to dare to dream big and go for it – no matter what! This was where I wanted to be.

"Shoot for the moon! Even if you miss, you will land among the stars."
– Les Brown

I remembered how my journey started. I got a job with a big sales and telemarketing company which was a big challenge for me. I had no experience, no higher education, and no special skills at all, plus I had a bad accent and medium English language skills.

"Use what talent you possess: the woods would be very silent
if no birds sang except those that sang best." - Van Dyke

Even though I had more weaknesses than strengths for the required job, I realized that what I did possess was more important, a burning desire, powerful intention, willingness to learn and master the skills required, and the determination to settle for nothing less than the best, relying on the faith, wisdom and creativity within myself to succeed.

At first, I was nervous, unconfident and uncomfortable to interact and sell to people I did not know, and had a terrible fear of rejection. The more I was trying to hide my bad accent, the more it appeared, leaving me speechless. For hours I felt the rejections of the potential clients and did not have courage to make calls, but soon I overcame them and became better. I thought, "I will persist until I succeed... period."

"The prizes of life are at the end of each journey, not near the beginning. Failure I may still encounter at the thousandth step, yet success hides behind the next bend in the road. Never will I know how close it lies unless I turn the corner." – Og Mandino

While my colleagues were confidently making many deals, I was struggling to make any at all, but I did not give up! I was determined to find my way to the top and I would not settle for nothing less than the best! I decided to improve and master the only little skills I had, no matter how small they were.

"Be faithful in small things because it's in them that your strength lies." – Mother Teresa

I carefully studied my best co-workers and learned their greatest skills and from that I created my own strategy. I spent countless hours learning my clients' buying psychology, different mentalities and personalities. I learned which mentalities were more receptive to my own and I learned to recognize my targeted clients fast, focus on the "winners" and eliminate the "time spenders." I leveraged my time, focused on results and was persistent.

At night, I visualized myself making big deals with grateful clients and would happily fall asleep achieving my goals. In the mornings I would wake up with joyful expectation and gratitude, knowing that my desires would be fulfilled and I was on my way. I had faith, belief and I knew that God is always with me, will hear my prayers and will make my dreams come true. I did not question how and when that would happen, I just let it go and let God to decide, calmly and joyfully expecting to receive it.

And miracles started to happen.

In less than 3 months I made the biggest deal that any of my colleagues had ever made. In less than a year, I became the top salesperson with totals greater than all of my other colleagues combined in the past 3 years. As an added bonus I bought myself a beautiful, luxury car – my treat to myself.

I ended up being the highest paid salesperson in the company and secured a unique agreement allowing me to work from my home. By now we were living in a beautiful apartment with a big terrace overlooking the ocean. I got to spend tons of time with my daughter and we were enjoying the life I'd envisioned just a year ago.

> *"It is funny about life: if you refuse to accept anything but the very best you will very often get it." - W. Maugham*

From a magical place with a precious view over the ocean, I'm sending a message to you:

"Dare to dream big! The only thing standing between you and your dream is your belief that it's possible and your willingness to go for it."

This shortened version of a chapter from **Sonja**'s upcoming book is based on her real life, which has been an amazing roller coaster ride of remarkable ups and downs with laughs and tears. If you enjoyed her story, you will truly love her book. Sonja loves to share her memories and feels fulfilled when her stories impact somebody's life positively! For free tips and secrets please visit www.MindsetToRiches.com. Contact her at SonjaBendz@gmail.com or +45 23450445 Denmark.

LIVE Your BEST Life Using the Ancient Wisdom of the Enneagram

MaryAnn Riddell

The key to living a full and balanced life is truly knowing and understanding your-self. We are all individual, unique and diverse. We all have habitually predictable ways of dealing with what life throws us.

Understanding your basic drives and core motivations gives you the insight and awareness to make wiser, conscious choices. Any sort of personal development path must take into account that there are different personality styles.

Have you ever wondered why some people can push your buttons, and others you feel an instant connection with immediately? You can have a situation that might incense one personality type yet not bother another type at all.

The result of this is that different personality types need different tools and advice for self-awareness, personal growth and enlightenment.

One of my most profound and life-transforming moments came when I was introduced to the Enneagram Personality Typing System. The following comes from *"The Wisdom of the Enneagram"* by Don-Richard Riso and Russ Hudson.

What is the Enneagram?

"Ennea" is Greek for nine and "gram" means model. The Enneagram is both a symbol, and a sophisticated yet simple personality system that describes nine different ways of looking at the world. In effect, nine individual different ways of thinking, interpreting, feeling and reacting to situations.

We all have a certain mix of all nine types in our overall personality with one particular style or pattern we return too. The number values of the Enneagram are neutral, with no type or number being better than another. When you know your Enneagram point or number, you can then be aware of the unconscious assumptions that motivate you to think, act and react the way you do.

Along with clarifying the strengths and limitations of your own worldview, with the Enneagram as a tool, you are in a position to understand why others act and respond to situations differently to you. Each of the nine world views is equally valid and you can understand how people see things from their unique perception, whether you agree with them or not.

Understanding the Enneagram gives you the tools to appreciate and value a viewpoint that is not your own. Indeed, understanding others from their perspective is an invaluable life-skill and tool which you will have forever.

So what type are you? You can find a free on-line test at www.insightshift.com.au right now.

The Nine Personality Types

Type One's - "The Reformer"- want to get things right and are principled, idealistic, self-controlled and perfectionists. They have a strong sense of mission or purpose and are adversaries for causes they believe in. The Basic Desire of the One is to be good and have integrity and they fear being bad, evil or corrupt. One's can become picky, resentful, critical, judgmental and compulsively organizing as they psychologically deteriorate.

Type Two's -"The Helper" - want to help others and are people pleasing, caring, and demonstrative. They are the warm-hearted empathetic types who are encouraging of others and able to see the good in people. The Basic desire of the Two's are to feel loved and their fear is of being unloved and not needed. Two's can become possessive and clingy and overdo giving to others as they psychologically deteriorate.

Type Three's - "The Achiever" - are driven, adaptable, success oriented, image conscious types. They are performance based and ambitious, self-assured, charming and others are motivated by their drive and energy levels. The Basic desire of the three's is to feel valued, and they fear that they have no personal value. Three's can become workaholics, competitive and narcissistic as they psychologically deteriorate.

Type Four's - "The Individualist" - are sensitive people who want to explore their true feelings and can be withdrawn, expressive and dramatic. They are seeking "sense of self" and can be very creative, intuitive and artistic, trying to make themselves unique. Their Basic desire is to create an identity out of their inner experiences and they fear having no significance. Four's can become dramatic, self-absorbed and temperamental as they psychologically deteriorate.

Type Five's - "The Investigator" - are the intense and cerebral types who are innovative, curious and perceptive. Fives are independent and want to understand the way the world works and are continually seeking knowledge. Their Basic desire is having value by being competent or having mastered something and fear being useless or incapable. They can become isolated, detached, anti-social, and eccentric as they psychologically deteriorate.

Type Six's - "The Loyalist" - are the committed, dutiful, loyal, responsible, courageous, trust-worthy type who is security oriented. Their Basic desire is to have security, certainty and support. Their Basic fear is of having no support or guidance and not being able to survive on their own. Six's can become dependent, defensive, superstitious, nervous, pessimistic and fear rejection as they go down the psychological health levels.

Type Seven's - "The Enthusiast" - are busy, versatile, spontaneous, and want the exciting possibilities and options. Seven's are exuberant, upbeat and can fear boredom. Seven's basic desire is to feel happy and fulfilled and they fear feeling deprived and trapped. Seven's can become acquisitive, scattered, and unproductive, and feel they are "missing out" as they psychologically deteriorate.

Type Eight's - "The Challenger" - are assertive, self-confident, dominating and confrontational, and want control. Eight's have enormous will power and are often the leaders of their world. The basic desire of the Eight is to protect themselves and their environment, and they fear being harmed or controlled by others. Eight's can begin to fear they don't have enough resources and become aggressively competitive and intimidating as they psychologically deteriorate.

Type Nine's - "The Peacemaker" - are easy going, self-effacing, receptive and reassuring and want to empathize with all the players and get the whole picture. Nine's can deny their own needs and can say yes when they mean no, avoiding conflict, trying to keep the peace. The Basic Desire of the Nine is to maintain their inner stability and peace of mind and they fear loss or separation. Nine's avoid conflict with others, become very stubborn, and live in a state of denial as they psychologically deteriorate.

Understanding what drives and motivates you allows you to create an inner awareness, where you have the option to make better choices for your life. Being able to then understand these driving forces in others, will allow you to see another's view from their unique perspective based on their Enneagram Type. Indeed, spiritual growth is a process where we are gentle, kind and patient with ourselves and others. The Enneagram will give you the tools and awareness to recognize your old predictable behavior patterns and to catch, or notice yourself before you repeat them. This pause gives you the option to respond, not react. You then have the option of replacing old behaviors with conscious, wiser choices.

You will experience an insight shift just knowing why another person reacts differently to you, and will gain the compassion and empathy to understand them from their perspective. This one thing can make all the difference in all of the relationships you have.

Please use and enjoy the profound insights of the wisdom of the Enneagram to LIVE your best life.

MaryAnn Riddell is a personal development coach specializing in creating work-life balance. MaryAnn uses the Enneagram as a powerful self-discovery tool with her clients, which gives them personal insights and awareness. MaryAnn runs 2-day workshops for women who want to "Live their BEST Life." MaryAnn and her husband Mark Birkbeck have the Enneagram Institute of Queensland and teach the Enneagram internationally using Riso-Hudson's Insight Approach. Take the free, fun personality test at www.insightshift.com.au or www.enneagramqueensland.com.

Be An Optimist At All Times

Brian Tracy

Everyone wants to be physically healthy. You want to be mentally healthy as well. The true measure of "mental fitness" is how optimistic you are about yourself and your life.

Below, you learn how to control your thinking in very specific ways so that you feel terrific about yourself and your situation, no matter what happens.

Control Your Reactions and Responses

There are three basic differences in the reactions of optimists and pessimists. The first difference is that the optimist sees a setback as temporary, while the pessimist sees it as permanent. The optimist sees an unfortunate event, such as an order that falls through or a sales call that fails, as a temporary event, something that is limited in time and that has no real impact on the future. The pessimist, on the other hand, sees negative events as permanent, as part of life and destiny.

Isolate the Incident

The second difference between the optimist and the pessimist is that the optimist sees difficulties as specific, while the pessimist sees them as pervasive. This means that when things go wrong for the optimist, he looks at the event as an isolated incident largely disconnected from other things that are going on in his life.

See Setbacks as Temporary Events

For example, if something you were counting on failed to materialize and you interpreted it to yourself as being an unfortunate event, but something that happens in the course of life and business, you would be reacting like an optimist. The pessimist, on the other hand, sees disappointments as being pervasive. That is, to him they are indications of a problem or shortcoming that pervades every area of life.

Don't Take Failure Personally

The third difference between optimists and pessimists is that optimists see events as external, while pessimists interpret events as personal. When things go wrong, the optimist will tend to see the setback as resulting from external factors over which one has little control.

If the optimist is cut off in traffic, for example, instead of getting angry or upset, he will simply downgrade the importance of the event by saying something like, "Oh, well, I guess that person is just having a bad day."

The pessimist on the other hand, has a tendency to take everything personally. If the pessimist is cut off in traffic, he will react as though the other driver has deliberately acted to upset and frustrate him.

Remain Calm and Objective

The hallmark of the fully mature, fully functioning, self-actualizing personality is the ability to be objective and unemotional when caught up in the inevitable storms of daily life. The superior person has the ability to continue talking to himself in a positive and optimistic way, keeping his mind calm, clear and completely under control. The mature personality is more relaxed and aware and capable of interpreting events more realistically and less emotionally than is the immature personality. As a result, the mature person exerts a far greater sense of control and influence over his environment, and is far less likely to be angry, upset, or distracted.

Take the Long View

Look upon the inevitable setbacks that you face as being temporary, specific and external. View the negative situation as a single event that is not connected to other potential events and that is caused largely by external factors over which you can have little control. Simply refuse to see the event as being in any way permanent, pervasive or indicative of personal incompetence of inability.

Resolve to think like an optimist, no matter what happens. You may not be able to control events but you can control the way you react to them.

Action Exercises

Now, here are three actions you can take immediately to put these ideas into action.

First, remind yourself continually that setbacks are only temporary, they will soon be past and nothing is as serious as you think it is.

Second, look upon each problem as a specific event, not connected to other events and not indicative of a pattern of any kind. Deal with it and get on with your life.

Third, recognize that when things go wrong, they are usually caused by a variety of external events. Say to yourself, "What can't be cured must be endured," and then get back to thinking about your goals.

Develop amazing self-confidence and be unstoppable in everything you do!

Think of all the things you could do if you enjoyed super levels of self-confidence... your career would be booming, offers would be flying your way, everyone would want to be with you. You would have more opportunities to find that "special someone."

Article exerpt reprinted with permission from *Entrepreneurial Success Articles* at www.BrianTracey.com.

Brian Tracy, Chairman and CEO of Brian Tracy International, specializes in the training and development of individuals and organizations to help them achieve personal and business goals faster and easier. Brian has consulted for more than 1,000 companies, addressed more than 4,000,000 people throughout the US, Canada and 40 other countries. He has written/produced more than 300 audio/video learning programs, including the worldwide best-selling Psychology of Achievement, which has been translated into more than 20 languages. For more information on Brian's amazing selection of audios, books and programs, visit www.BrianTracey.com today.

LIVING A LIFE WITH PURPOSE

HOW TO REMOVE STRESS AND EMBRACE SUCCESS

Wendy Moore

I never knew what I wanted to be when I grew up. So when I graduated high school, Dad did what all good Dad's do and sent me to secretarial college. From there I secured an administrative role at a major Australian bank and my climb up the corporate ladder had begun!

Within two years I'd met my future (now ex) husband, and when his work transferred him to Tokyo I followed. Reality soon hit. A towering blond Aussie living in a land of small people with no friends or language, I certainly stood out, but for all the wrong reasons.

The Tokyo stint ended, we headed home, got married and I became a secretary at a major law firm. My life was miserable. I hated my job with its hierarchical culture where few people spoke to subordinates. Home life was also dismal as I quickly realized my marriage was a big mistake, but we persisted.

Professionally, I happily moved from the law firm to the IT department of a large mining company where my life dramatically changed. Everyone was so happy and inclusive. This astounded me and I relished my new environment. I was inspired. Within a month I had enrolled in a six year part-time computing degree and loved my work. The love however didn't carry through at home where things deteriorated. Within two months of my starting the new job we had split.

I moved back home with my parents while I looked for my first property. I knew absolutely nothing about real estate and it showed. This was in 1997, at what turned out to be the start of a massive property boom in Melbourne.

Auction day – my very first auction! Mum and Dad came along as Dad was to bid on my behalf to ensure I didn't get emotional and bid way over my budget. To my horror, dad's first bid was $7,500 over my reserve price! Gulp. I was about to become a homeowner!

Life was progressing nicely. I was enjoying my job and studying for my computing degree part-time. Then in 2000 life turned again when the mining company was swallowed up by a much larger player and we were all made redundant. The worst part was the feeling of total lack of control. It was not pleasant and is one I never wish to experience again.

After a short break, I joined a small Australian IT company where I met my future partner and really started to drive my IT career.

I'd fast tracked my degree, with no summer break for three straight years, to finish in just 5 years. What a relief! My evenings and weekends were again mine.

Property had become my passion. I'd started to attend seminars and read everything I could about property investing. My next purchase was in October 2003 at the height of the Melbourne boom. Within weeks the market went flat. I'd purchased at the peak of the market and, despite doing all the research, I still got it wrong!

I purchased a property 5 minutes drive from my home and ended up being in a negative cash flow situation. I'd gone over my budget (again!) and fundamentally made my investment decision on emotion rather than the facts and figures. As a result, life became a real struggle. Mind you, no one would have known as I didn't tell a soul. Having to take things back to the store because you need that money to pay your bills is a very humbling experience. My belt was pulled in extra tight for quite a few years.

Even so, I still loved property and in 2005 I joined a mentoring program that was set to ignite a massive fire within me. I was on holiday in Paris the day of registration and I sat up until 4 am so I didn't miss out. The number of enrollees actually brought the website down, but I got in and I was on my way.

The IT company I consulted for was taken over by an Indian conglomerate in 2004 and immediately the culture changed. I stuck it out for eighteen months, but eventually joined another small Australian IT company, just prior to enrolling in the property mentoring program. I'd finally made it to the very top of the corporate IT world, managing $45 million budgets with a six-figure income.

Within six months I had purchased 10 properties and loved every minute of it. I was still working full time and in every spare minute I had I would research property into the wee hours of the morning.

I finally bit the bullet and sold the property I'd purchased three years earlier as it did not fit with my overall strategy. I lost money, but the lessons learned proved invaluable.

In mid 2006, I read Kim Kyosaki's book "Rich Woman." This was to prove a huge catalyst for what was to come. Kim suggests that women should seek out female investing groups and if you can't find one, create one.

My property investing was very successful and I approached my employer about working a four day week. Persistence paid off and in August 2006 my four day weeks began.

In September 2006, while I was listening to one of my inspirational CD's, little did I know that my life was about to change forever. Brendan Nichols, a mentor, was discussing 'significance' and asked "What are you here to do?" The epiphany that followed struck me like a thunderbolt. I realized my purpose is to educate and empower others. In that moment it all became so clear.

Shortly thereafter I established Affluencia.com, Australia's leading property investing website for women. Our first property meeting was held in October 2006. *Affluencia*, Latin for abundance, truly represents what I am looking to inspire in other women.

Throughout the final 12 months as a project manager for the IT company, I had started to experience health problems, and headaches plagued me almost daily. I realized I was suffering from massive stress. So much so, I eventually could not get out of bed to go to work without physically throwing up.

Working 4 days a week had opened the door and now my epiphany had flung it wide open. I had experienced such a mental shift that each morning, the very thought of doing something totally misaligned with my purpose would cause a physical reaction.

A visit to my doctor confirmed what I already knew. I was suffering gut wrenching stress and needed a lifestyle change. I resigned in December 2006 and within two weeks all the health problems I had been experiencing for over 12 months disappeared. I was miraculously cured!

Overnight I became a full time investor reaping the associated financial rewards and lifestyle. In less than two years I had acquired a multimillion dollar portfolio around Australia, based on positive cash flow.

The absolute freedom you feel when you follow your heart and devote yourself to your passion cannot be adequately expressed in words. It is like your soul has been set free.

My absolute passion is to educate and empower as many women as possible on the road to financial freedom, to encourage them to find and follow their passion and to live an inspired life. I do this through Affluencia.com, one woman – and investment – at a time.

Wendy Moore's high powered, highly paid and highly stressful IT position was making her sick – literally. An epiphany inspired her to throw in her job and follow her real passion - property investing, and educating and empowering other women. She formed Affluencia – a women's only property investing network that's kicking goals for her and her motivated ladies.

For empowering property tips and your inspiring FREE Property eBook valued at $25, visit www.Affluencia.com today!

CHANGE YOUR MINDSET
AND CHANGE YOUR LIFE

YOU CAN HAVE IT ALL – IT'S YOURS TO TAKE!

Nikhil Rughani

I woke up this morning, ready to write this thinking, "This is exciting! I can tell people that they really *can* have it all – happiness, health, wealth, love and an exciting drive for an incredible life."

I'm living proof! Life really is great for me, and I'm really thankful that I've got so much.

Here I am, with a wonderful wife, a supportive family, feeling energetic and invincible, and with wealth that is growing day by day. Every day I feel a sense of purpose for myself and I have the confidence and inspiration to really burst beyond any barrier that comes before me.

Over the last 5 years my life has really changed. Looking back on it, I really am proud of my achievements in getting where I am today. I have much more to accomplish, but I am already taking it on.

Yet life for me wasn't always this great.

Having struggled to graduate from university a few years earlier, I was working in a technical support job for the last 3 years and I hated it. I used to tell myself that I liked helping people and that's why I took on this job. Initially that was true, but now hardly a day would go past when I wouldn't be cursing my customers after every call. I had been turned down for every promotion and my self-esteem was at an all time low. I was single, but everyone around me was in an awesome relationship with really fun people. In an attempt to make myself feel better, I would spend a lot of money on useless items that entertained me for a few days, but then the novelty wore off. Credit cards were becoming my savior when money ran out. While the credit cards were good, the bills weren't, and I racked up massive debts on numerous credit cards.

This was life – except I was not living, just merely existing.

At that time I decided that I would become a psychic. I'd always had an interest in the mystical, and I knew that I would still be able to help people out. As if I was undertaking some noble cause, I felt that in helping people be happy, I would be happy. So I found myself a famous psychic who agreed to teach me the mystical arts one-on-one. After my training and a lot of practice, I became a part-time psychic helping people clear the cobwebs of confusion, and giving them direction. While I liked giving people advice, it really made things worse for me. Here I was telling them how they could have awesome lives, but *my* life was far from awesome! How hypocritical! I decided that I would take a self-development course to get a sense of direction of what I wanted in my life. The good thing about this course was that I got a temporary boost to my self-confidence, but it didn't last. CD's, books, seminars and courses didn't have any sustained affect on me either.

One day, I was expressing my frustration at life to a friend of mine, and she suggested that I take a vacation. "Break away from the routine and just do nothing", she told me. My first reaction was "Uh, no. How do I explain to people that I'm going away to do nothing?" But then I thought, "Hey, just do it. I've done seminars and listened to CD's, surely I've learned about doing something for myself and not worrying about what other people think! Besides, it might be fun!" And so I did it. I came off my shift at work, went straight to the airport, and took a vacation on an island off the south-coast of Australia. I literally did nothing! If you've never done this before, I highly recommend it!

During this period of doing nothing, I did do a lot of soul searching. I got to think about the good things I wanted for my life, and I decided that I'd had enough of the sorrow and misery. On the flight home I decided that if I wanted change, I had to take the first step. I went to work and tendered my resignation. I had no job to go to, but I still wanted to work somewhere where I could help people as I actually did enjoy helping them out. The next week I ended up getting work with the government, assisting people with their difficult situations.

My vacation thinking gained momentum and I realized that I needed to keep focusing on me if I wanted to be happy, find a loving relationship, and wanted to be wealthy.

A couple of months later I got introduced to a lovely young lady and before I knew it we were in a beautiful relationship. Romeo and Juliet had nothing on us! A year later we got married and started our life together.

After my wedding, I decided to leave my government job and went to work in the recruitment industry so that I could learn some new skills, yet I still had one thing on my mind – financial freedom. All my life, I had been resistant to money, but now I was ready to blast through my debts to create a life of abundance and prosperity. A promotion and relocation allowed me and my wife to spend the time together and carry out a plan for financial independence. In 18 months we eliminated all our credit card debt and built up a substantial amount of savings. I'd never been able to save that much money before! In addition, the application of a "success mindset" decreased my stress levels and proportionately increased my level of achieving much more, and a whole lot faster as well. I also started to focus on my health. Our efforts in eating well and exercising regularly pushed our energy levels up significantly. I was getting a sense of what life was really meant to be like – and it was beautiful. It was exciting! It was unbelievable!

Because my life had become so powerful, people around me started shining too. My desire to help people started taking form – for once I was inspiring other people! They wanted to be like me!

I knew that this was what I was meant to do – show people how they can have it all. To go from simply existing, to living a breathtaking life. Through a series of mentoring programs, seminars and courses, I help people get the life they crave.

Who doesn't want to be happy and in a beautiful relationship? Who doesn't want to be in control of their finances and be extremely healthy? Who doesn't want to feel great, and be a positive influence on people around them?

You just need to look inside and start doing what you *truly* want. Once you start doing that, with a bit of persistence and support, your life will quickly become amazing and you will live your dreams, I promise you. If I can do it, so can *you*. And *you will!*

Nikhil Rughani, success mentor extraordinaire, provides powerful solutions to propel *your* life to beyond just the next level. Through Nikhil's unparalleled programs, *you* will unlock your ability to realize *your* dreams and ensure that *your* life is phenomenal. Go to www.NikhilRughani.com and discover your purpose, develop a powerful attitude, control your finances, get your health on track and add some "zing" to your love life. Download your free tip-sheet and start creating an awesome life.

Always Blessings

Marie Diane Schilly

I am blessed. I wake up each day grateful for how abundant life is and continues to be. Yes, I have material prosperity, yet more importantly to me, I have family and friends who truly love me, terrific health, energy to enjoy my interests, and dogs who share all my experiences. I treasure my career as an Abundance Coach that I love with passion, especially guiding my clients who continue to expand their own abundance and achieve their dreams. My life is a continually changing kaleidoscope filled with wealth, life balance, love, and joy. I awake happy, looking forward to the day. I end my day recording the day's gifts in my gratitude journal. I feel so incredibly blessed.

Was it always this way? No, of course not. If so, my story would be very dull, don't you think? I had to learn first how my beliefs and emotions were creating my life, then how to attract abundance for myself, and subsequently how to help others change their beliefs and emotions to achieve their goals and dreams. The last few years in particular, have been a life-changing journey -- from being financially comfortable, to financially destitute, and, ultimately, returning to financial and personal abundance beyond my wildest dreams. Along the way, I learned a tremendous amount about myself and how my thought processes, that reflects my deepest beliefs and emotions, were subconsciously directing what I created in my life.

I have always been an innately happy person. So how did I go from being a happy, successful, financially comfortable person, to one who had no money and who was borrowing from the "Mom Bank" to survive? For starters, I forgot that happy people create their own happy endings.

The journey to learn about creating and sustaining abundance began when I was holidaying in France. During that long-planned trip,

I had one of those horrid feelings of something gone terribly wrong. I even had a strong premonition to call my stockbroker, but I did not, using the excuse of the time difference. Really, I was doing "creative avoidance". I returned home to learn that all my money and reserves had been lost. My financial wealth was eliminated overnight. I filed for bankruptcy, exacerbating my feelings of failure, incompetence, and embarrassment.

I replaced happiness and joy with fear, anger, sadness, and blame. This situation had to be someone else's fault, didn't it? I would never, ever, in a million years, have put myself in this situation! I focused on my lack of money, what I had lost, and how my life had changed. My whole picture of success was linked to money and what I thought it provided. I completely overlooked all that I still had in my life: a supportive family, fabulous friends, a home I loved, a job I adored, and my health. My stress level increased the more my money decreased.

I remembered my affirmations, to think positively, and to write daily in my gratitude journal. If someone listened to my words, I sounded like I was focused on all that I still had in my life. I had learned that much from the courses I had taken. Yet, deep within and unspoken, I was really focusing on lack – everything that was missing from my life. I was depressed and consumed with sadness. The joyful face I wore in public was my method to delude myself along with others: a "fake it until you make it" approach.

One thing I have come to love about myself is that I will go to great lengths to be certain that I learn everything I need to know about a situation. Remember the kaleidoscope, and how when you turn the wheel, the picture changes? I explored my sense of lack from every angle, turning that kaleidoscope wheel frequently over several years.

What began as a financial loss, accelerated into other nuances of loss. I lost my job, many friendships dissolved, prized possessions were sold, my retirement funds were cashed in, my home was sold to avoid foreclosure, and ultimately my car was sold to cover medical bills. I can be, at times, a stubborn student!

What was most frustrating is that I know I am an intelligent person, yet I was unable to figure out how to change the direction my life was taking. During this time, a friend paid for a course in manifesting techniques. What an amazing gift! Of course, I was unaware of the significance of this gift at that time. Remember, I still focused on lack. However, that course began a journey to explore how my beliefs and emotions created my reality.

As I diligently explored my lack consciousness, I replaced those limiting beliefs and emotions with ones that held pictures of prosperity, love, and joy. My happiness returned along with my love of life. I discovered the importance of feeling appreciation and gratitude – for everything -- no matter how small or insignificant.

I learned the magnitude of focusing on what it feels like to have what you want in your life. Whenever a feeling of lack or loss arose, I directed my attention and energy to what it felt like to have more of what I wanted instead of what I lacked: more friends, fun, free time, income, peace and quiet, joy, love, and happiness.

I began receiving unexpected gifts of money at times when I wondered how I was going to pay rent, put tires on my car, or buy groceries. Friendships blossomed and relationships healed. My health recovered and income increased. I was able to repay the "Mom Bank" more quickly than I expected.

Five truths I learned from my journey:

1. Forgive yourself for choices and decisions made.

2. Ask your inner-self for help, and listen for the answers.

3. Be open to what comes without attachment to the outcome.

4. Feel, truly feel, grateful and appreciative for everything.

5. Remember: "Always blessings; never losses."

"Always blessings. Never losses." Four simple words that refocused my life. I wish I could take credit for these words. The words were part of a John Edwards program seen by a dear friend. Although I cannot take credit for the words, I can take credit for the insight and changes those words brought to my life.

Abundance, to me, is more than financial; it includes love, friendships, relationships, knowledge, health, life balance, passion, joy, and happiness. As an Abundance Coach, I passionately share everything I have learned to help others create the life of their dreams. Together, we go about "Untying Your Not's™", looking at the beliefs and emotions blocking your prosperity, and replacing those obstacles with ones that accelerate what you want in your life.

I am blessed to again be waking every day happily – because I know, truly know, that all of this life is an abundant blessing, never losses. The kaleidoscope wheel always shifts. When I am unable to see the blessing in the situation, I turn the wheel until I see the gift.

Know that what I have done, you can too! My wish for you is abundant blessings in every area of your life.

Marie Schilly is an international Abundance Coach, Certified Counseling Intuitive®, and successful businesswoman. Marie joyfully and passionately guides others in how to attain prosperity, happiness, love, joy, and balance in every area of life. Marie empowers you with tailored techniques that are uniquely easy to implement, engaging, and fun. Visit her website today for your free audio download to attract abundance.

You can contact Marie through her website: www.OutrageouslyAbundant.com or by email at Marie@OutrageouslyAbundant.com.

THE LIFE SAVING PROPERTIES
OF THE JOYGASM

Anne Rycroft

"I hate my life, I hate my life, I hate my life."

These are the thoughts that used to run through my head every day, from the moment I awoke with tears in my eyes, until the moment I fell into a deep, exhausted sleep as my head hit the pillow at the end of another long and miserable day.

Like me, you might wonder what caused these thoughts to develop. My life appeared to be good. I was married, I had a home and I had a great career. My sons were growing older and so I had more time to pursue my own interests... sounds good, right? And yet I was so unhappy with my life and felt like it was totally out of control.

Do you, like I did, feel this way from time to time? You might feel that life is hard. Maybe you believe that money is hard to get or that you have to work hard to make your marriage work. I too, believed all these things and more.

I was unhappy in my marriage, but believed that you have to work hard to have a good marriage. I was loath to give up and admit that I had 'failed.'

So my life became a habit of unhappiness. A habit of waking up, going to work, coming home, complaining about how bad work was that day, eating dinner, falling asleep in front of whatever was on the television screen, and then finally waking in time to go to bed, all the while hearing that little voice in my head repeating 'I hate my life' over and over again.

And then my life changed. I left my marriage, sold our home, set myself and my sons up in a much smaller home, but it was enough. I was going to take control of my life and stop feeling the way I had been. I discovered the world of self-improvement and started to devour books of that genre.

Then along came the JOYgasm and my life would never be the same again.

Through books by authors such as Dr. Wayne Dyer, Esther and Jerry Hicks and others, I was beginning to open up to the possibility that I could be happy, and that all I had to do to be happy was to 'change my mind' and choose to be happy. Was it really that easy, I wondered? How could it be so effortless? I mean, hadn't I already established that life was hard?

I began to learn about the benefits of appreciating what I did have. As I appreciated what I already had in my life, I began to love it as well. I began to love myself, my life and all the things and people in my life. It occurred to me that the more I appreciated what I had, the more wonderful and exciting things that started to come into my life for me to appreciate.

I had discovered one of the secrets of life: the quickest way from wherever you are now to happiness, is through appreciation. Appreciation of what you are currently living, while dreaming of better in the future, allows the dreamt-of future to become a reality.

My daily habits began to change. Instead of the previous drudgery, I woke up excited and eager to start the new day. Oh what wonders awaited me? I would start every day appreciating the fact that I had enjoyed a good night's sleep, that I had a soft comfy bed to sleep in. I appreciated that I had sheets to cover my body and keep it warm, and the pillow to cradle my head while I dreamt. And the day would go on with me appreciating everything: my job, my car, the money that I took out of my wallet to pay for milk on the way home … even the wallet! I appreciated everything and anything, including what life had thus far thrown at me and yes, I even grew to appreciate all the experiences of my marriage and my ex-husband. And I ended every day with appreciation for all that I had experienced during that particular day.

It was becoming very obvious to me and to those around me that I was happy. I had found my happiness through appreciation. I wanted to put a name to my new habit and JOYgasm just seemed to fit, as it was allowing me to feel such joy and pure happiness, and had even started me back on the road to loving myself, right where I had taken the left path instead of the right in the 'fork in the road.'

The word JOYgasm has been defined as a colloquial term for a feeling of extreme joy and you can hear Jim Carrey as the Joker in *Batman Forever* (1995) utter it as he destroys Batman's cave. Even though the actors actions are what most would consider negative, the joy he feels in his actions is way beyond what would be considered normal, hence the use of the term JOYgasm.

I offer you the following sample of a JOYgasm in appreciation of you, of me, and of loving ourselves fully and unconditionally. You will derive the most benefit from these words if you sit for a moment and completely focus on the feelings of each part, take in each word and feel the love it holds for you.

"I am perfect just the way I am. I am loved. I am love. I love. I get to choose what I want and where I will go from here. I can choose something better right now. All I have to do is change my mind and I know I can do that because I have done it before. I was perfect when I came into the world and I am still perfect; that does not change. I was created in God's image and He is perfect, so I also am perfection. I am perfect and all is as it should be right now and if I want any of it to change, it can. All I have to do is change my mind and follow the path that leads to my heart's desire. Love is beautiful. I am beautiful. I am good. I love me. I love me. I love me. I am love and I give love."

For me, learning of the JOYgasm has been nothing short of a miracle. I have been able to change my life from one of despair and hopelessness, to one of love, joy, happiness and fun, fun, fun. I now have a happy life where money flows to me effortlessly, where creativity is the norm, where love is open and unconditional, where spirituality and growth is easy, and where my dreams are coming true every single day.

I've gone from being an unhappy, empty shell of a woman, to a fun, loving, joyful mother, business owner, author, public speaker, 100% into life, puddle jumping, happy woman in a few short years. And all I had to do was change my mind and make the choice to be happy.

If I can do it, then there is nothing stopping you from doing it. Make the choice to be happy and live with a constant sense of wonder and appreciation for what you have right now. I know that you can have everything that you can imagine... and so much more.

To your happiness.

Anne Rycroft, Joy coach, author and speaker, developed the JOYgasm after experiencing a great shift in her mindset and life, while practicing the art of appreciation. The JOYgasm is a powerful blast of appreciation. Get yours by visiting www.dailyjoygasm.com and signing up for your free daily JOYgasm. But be warned: the JOYgasm may cause sudden and frequent bouts of happiness. Visit www.stepuptojoy.com for more resources to help you find your happiness, one step at a time.

Your Calling is Calling

Michelle Kulp

My Pivotal Moment - On October 23, 1992, I met a man by the name of Billy Ray Cyrus (U.S. Country Music Singer and Actor), who literally changed the entire direction of my life. I strongly believe it was my spiritual destiny to meet him. In 1992, I was at a very dark and desperate place in my life. My marriage had ended, I was living paycheck to paycheck with bankruptcy looming, I was raising 3 small children on my own, I was fired from my job, my brother was diagnosed with Aids and was dying and I was having severe panic attacks.

Music that Spoke to my Soul – In 1992, at a neighbor's suggestion, I began listening to Billy Rays' hit song *"Achy Breaky Heart."* This was a stretch for me because up until then I had only listened to "Rock-n-Roll." I became hooked, quickly, and many nights blasted the song and escaped my very much-stressed out life!

So when that same neighbor came to me two week's later to let me know that Billy Ray was playing at a concert on October 23, 1992 at the Patriot Center in Virginia, I knew I had to go. It was also my birthday. The thoughts, "Billy Ray is playing on my birthday for a reason… and he has something very important to tell me" came to me. Perhaps all the stress was causing me to be delusional, but I honestly believed that I was going to meet Billy Ray, and that he had a message for me.

No Doubts, but Lots of Obstacles – I was 100% certain I would meet Billy Ray, and because of this I made a simple plan: I would enlist my good friend Jackie to go to the concert with me, then after the concert we would get a roadie to get us backstage passes to meet Billy Ray. Also, I wanted to stand out from the crowd so I decided to wear a red Spandex dress and red pumps.

After four attempts to get backstage, Jackie and I were kicked out and told we would be arrested if we returned. We immediately went to Plan B, which was to wait for Billy Ray to come out of the concert hall and follow the limo to the hotel. We stayed in our car, ready for flight, and when he emerged, I simply drove like a maniac so I didn't lose sight of him!

I would NOT give up! – We followed the limo to the Hilton Hotel, where Billy Ray's bodyguard, Steve, was taking Billy Ray up to his hotel room through a side door at the hotel. Luckily for me, all the women who were also following the limo jumped out of their cars and started running toward the side door of the hotel. My friend jumped out of our moving car and went to tell Billy Ray to wait for me because it was my birthday. I parked the car and ran to the elevator where Billy Ray was standing. He autographed a t-shirt I'd brought, and the bodyguard snapped a picture of us. Before I could do or say anything, bodyguard Steve abruptly pushed everyone out of the elevator and told us, "Billy Ray is going upstairs for the night. Good night!" About 10 minutes later, after everyone left, we came back in.

We got in the elevator and started our search. Before too long we saw Steve going into a room on the 12th floor. I was so excited because I knew my dream was going to come true! But as soon as Steve saw us heading toward Billy Ray's room, he threatened to have hotel security remove us. The more I tried to argue with him, the more irritated he became so hesitantly, I left and headed back toward the elevator.

I couldn't give up! I stood in the elevator searching for ideas and noticed a plaque with room numbers on it. Looking across the hall I saw a house phone. I picked it up, dialed the last number on the plaque and Voila! Billy Ray answered. When I told him who was calling, Billy Ray replied, "You mean the girl in the red dress?" Wow! He remembered me. He also said if there hadn't been all those women downstairs, he would have invited me to his hotel room for some Chinese food. I told him, "I'm here now!"

Better Late, than Never – For the next few hours (he was a complete gentleman), we discussed family, relationships, God, his music, etc. I told Billy Ray my rather desperate life story, at which point he looked deeply into my eyes and said something to me that changed my whole life.

Dreams – Billy Ray asked me "What are your Dreams?" to which I quickly replied, "I don't have any dreams, my life's about survival." Billy Ray assured me I had a dream, and that I needed to go out and discover what my dream was and never, ever give up on that dream.

One year, one small book and one BIG Dream! - I took Billy Ray's advice and went searching for this elusive dream, but it wasn't so easy to find. Finally about a year later, I found it in a book called *How to Find Your Mission in Life* by Richard Bolles. One sentence uncovered my dream—"What do you love to do where you lose all sense of time?" I knew the answer – I loved to write! When I wrote, five hours seemed like five minutes.

One Road leads to Many Others –In 1993 I started writing. I joined writing groups, attended conferences, freelanced for a newspaper and read everything I could find on the subject. This led me to becoming a motivational speaker, workshop leader, author and life coach.

In 1999, after 15 years in the legal field, I left my secure job with lots of benefits to follow my dreams. More importantly, I left that job because I felt unfulfilled and spiritually drained at the end of every day. Moreover, it sapped my creativity and imagination from me. And on top of that – I was broke!

Living my Dream - I now live my dream life. I work 20-25 hours a week and make a 6-figure income. I love what I do and would never have imagined this life all those years ago. I talk to so many unhappy people who are killing themselves just to pay the bills, and I want to help them improve the quality of their lives so they can live their dreams too! I teach women worldwide how to become 6-figure winners and how to create a life they absolutely love.

John O'Donohue, Irish poet and Catholic Scholar, reminds us, *"To be born is to be chosen. No one is here by accident. Each one of us was sent here for a special destiny."*

I believe you are reading these words because your *"Calling is Calling."* A calling is asking the question, "What do I really want out of life"? Your dreams await you. Don't deny your heart or your dreams any longer.

So take a leap of faith and follow your dreams! You never know where they might lead.

Michelle Kulp is a single parent of three who left a 15 year career in the legal field to follow her dreams. She is now a dynamic motivational speaker, writer, coach and 6 figure woman. Michelle has a passion for sharing with others how to create a life of prosperity, abundance, and happiness. Michelle has created a number of successful online courses.

To receive your Free Gifts, please visit her website at www.BecomeA6FigureWoman.com or email her at Michelle@BecomeA6FigureWoman.com.

CHOOSE TO BE SUCCESSFUL

Karen Leslie

As I sit here writing this, I feel blessed. I'm married to the man of my dreams, living in a house that I love, in the place where we chose to live. We make money while we sleep in many countries across the world and it feels amazing to be able to say that! It's a long way from where I grew up in a terraced house in South East London, where I managed to fail to get into University.

When we look back on our lives we can see choices that were life changing. For me a huge choice was getting into personal development. I know that some of you may groan when you hear those words, but personal development means different things to different people. For me it meant getting rid of the things that held me back. I was like one of the sailors who set out to discover the New World when they thought the world may be flat. I'd sail off with fantastic intentions, and then as I got closer and closer to where I wanted to be, I'd turn back. I'd tell myself that I couldn't do it "because......." There were many different reasons, or now as I look at it, excuses that I would tell myself. I was actually setting myself up for failure!

As I was reading personal growth books and going to seminars, I realized that I envied the people that had the disadvantages. I know how crazy that sounds! I thought that if only I could have had that drawback then I would be where they are today. They were lucky to have had those obstacles – and then I heard what I had just thought! How could I think that they were lucky to struggle against hardships? And then I realized what the matter was. They had physical, tangible reasons why they should not have been successful. Maybe it was poverty, a bad childhood, but I didn't have any of those things. My parents are still together and happily married after many years. If we were poor, I hadn't noticed. I never had to go without food, and at school we could still afford the school uniform whereas others couldn't. I've had some abuse from being bi-racial, but nothing worth writing about. So when I've had it relatively easy, why was I wishing that I'd had some challenges? Because I thought that people with a disadvantage had an excuse to be unsuccessful, and I wanted one too. But guess what? There are no excuses for being unsuccessful. I'm serious. The only excuses actually exist in our heads.

That little voice that says,

"Can you really do that?

Do you really deserve that?

Will anyone listen to you?

Will anyone read what you write?"

That little voice in your head is the only thing that holds you back. And if you're thinking that you don't have a little voice – that's the little voice!

The only real disadvantage I have is the same one that everyone else has, and that is that sometimes I listen to that little voice inside my head when it's saying negative things.

There is some good news and bad news about that 'little voice.' The bad news is that you can never switch it off; it's just part of what makes us human. The good news is that once you become aware of it, you can choose to ignore it. Why choose to ignore it? Because deep down, really deep down, you want to be happy and successful, and by successful I mean fulfilled in whatever you choose to do. For some that may mean the big house with the expensive car sitting outside; for others it may mean doing a job that they love, or spending time with family and friends. Whatever your little voice is saying right now, about whether you deserve it or not, trust me you do. You can add so much to the world around you and you are probably not even aware of it. If you don't believe me try smiling at someone. Not only do you feel good doing it, you make someone else feel better.

When you realize that your little voice has said something negative, just question it. Ask yourself "Is this true?" If it tells you that you can't do something, just change your thinking to "I can learn how to …." In some cases you know that you can do it, but fear holds you back. Question your fear and find out if it's real since in most cases it's not.

My husband will tell you that ten years ago he couldn't have imagined that we would be where we are now. I used to get up, have breakfast, go to work, come home, eat, watch television, go to bed and repeat. I was trapped in the 9-5 rat race and I didn't know there was anything else. Sure I saw people living another lifestyle on television, but they were somehow different. But when I got involved with self-improvement, I realized there were so many different opportunities that I wasn't aware of. There was property investing, share trading, internet marketing and so much more. If I learned how to do even one of these, I could actually change my life and do whatever I wanted to do. I tried for a few years and didn't get anywhere fast. Why? I hadn't realized that my little voice was working against me – a kind of self-sabotage. All of these things work as long as you have the belief that they will work for you. It's not 'seeing is believing' - it's 'believing is seeing.'

Now I surround myself with positive people, and immerse myself in self improvement so that little voice doesn't stand a chance. We now have a property portfolio with a value in excess of 7 figures, make profits from shares in any market, and earn money while we sleep.

In July 2006 I joined Success University, which is the largest growing personal achievement online University. The courses are from some of the top speakers and authors in personal growth. It was the answer to what I had been looking for, since I could access it 24/7 from anywhere in the world with an internet connection. In December 2006 I became the first female Director in Europe. I'd been involved with network marketing company's years before, and I hadn't achieved anything. What's the difference? Simple. Personal development takes away any excuses that you have built up over the years. It gets deep down to the successful, wonderful you inside and sets you free. Free to be whom you want to be, to do what you want to do, and to have what you want to have.

Remember that when you hear that little negative voice. It's just you trying to hold yourself back, because there are no excuses and you can achieve whatever you want in life. Just choose to be successful – it's that simple.

Karen Leslie, professional network marketer, personal development consultant and thriving property investor, has successfully run her own business for over ten years. She loves empowering people to be the best that they can be through her mindset coaching. To receive her free newsletter "Changing Your Mind", sign up at her website at http://www.Money-Magnets.net or contact her via email at karen@Money-Magnets.net.

Finding Big Love is Possible at any Age

Arielle Ford

Is it your dream to find a soul mate? A life-partner who will love, cherish and adore you?

As someone who didn't meet and marry my soul mate until I was 44, I learned a lot along the way about what does and doesn't work in the world of love and romance.

Here's what I know for sure: finding true love is possible for anyone at *any* age if you're willing to prepare yourself, on all levels, to become a magnet for love.

This wonderful Universe of ours is set up to deliver the people and things we draw to us that is consistent with our personal belief system. If you don't believe you will ever find the ONE, then, guess what? You get to be right …you probably won't.

If, however, you learn to believe that the ONE is not only out there, but is ALSO LOOKING FOR YOU, then true love can be yours.

Do you hold one or more of the following beliefs?

- I'm too old.
- I'm too fat.
- I'm too damaged.
- I have too much baggage.
- I'm too successful.
- I'm not successful enough.
- All the good ones are taken.
- Nobody I wants, wants me.

These are just knee-jerk excuses to keep you stuck. There is plenty of evidence that love is available to EVERYONE, regardless of age, weight, income or any other feeble excuse.

One day something happened that really solidified in me the belief for me that my soul mate was out there… somewhere.

I was watching Oprah and she had Barbra Streisand on the show. Barbra had recently fallen in love with James Brolin and I remember thinking, "Here is this super-wealthy, ultra famous diva….how many men could be a match for her?" And then I realized, "If God could find somebody for her, then I'll be a piece of cake!"

I knew in that moment, <u>with absolute certainty</u> that if the Universe had the perfect man for Barbra Streisand, then my soul mate was definitely out there. I also knew that I needed to prepare myself on every level to magnetize him into my life.

At that point in my life I was working from home, and the only men I ever met were the mailman, the UPS man, the Sparkletts water delivery guy….and most of them were already married!

I began using everything I had ever learned about manifestation, psychology, spirituality, and the Law of Attraction and applied it to my love life. My intentions became crystal clear while I simultaneously cleared out the clutter in my house AND in my heart. I learned and invented techniques, rituals, visualizations and prayers that helped me prepare my body, mind, spirit and home for an amazing relationship. And they worked.

Within six months of getting serious about manifesting my soul mate, I met my husband, Brian, who has exceeded all of my desires and expectations. He was and is everything I ever wished for.

What if I told you that it's not your job to know HOW your soul mate is going to appear? What if I told you it's only your job to be ready, willing and open to love. Think about it this way: you really don't know where air comes from, but you do believe that it's always there for you, right?

The same is true for love. It's there for you. It's always been there for you. You just need to remember the love that you *are* and once you do, the Universe will deliver to you the perfect soul mate.

The basic Law of Attraction states that you will attract to you those things that match your state of belief.

Believing that your soul mate is out there is critical to the preparation of manifestation.

I believe that the Universe is always mirroring back to us our beliefs about ourselves and the world. If we believe the world is a loving and friendly place, then most of the time that will be our experience. But, if we believe the world is a chaotic, stressful and fearful place, then that becomes our reality. So, believing and knowing that your soul mate is out there is the most important part of the formula.

Prior to meeting Brian ten years ago, I had a daily ritual in which I would light several candles at sunset, put on my favorite CD of Gregorian chants and sit in my big, cozy chair. With my eyes closed I would drop into the feeling of remembering the joy of having my soul mate in my life. I would experience these wonderful feelings in every part of my body KNOWING that he was on the way. There were days when the thought that he was very late did cross my mind, but I would just let those thoughts go and get back into a state of grace.... feeling and knowing that his arrival was assured.

To manifest your soul mate here are the ten top things to do and remember:

- Be the loving person that you are. Find ways to express more love to everyone in your life.

- Live in the knowingness that you are in a loving, committed relationship.

- Live that truth every day as you savor the waiting for your beloved to arrive.

- Create a "vision map" of your romantic vision and look at it daily.

- Write a list of the most important qualities your soul mate will possess.

- Heal your heart of any past hurts that will prevent you from magnetizing big love.

- Clear out the clutter in your home and create space for your beloved (especially in your closets).

- Create an altar in the relationship corner of your home.

- Listen to your intuition to take action when opportunities present themselves.

- Fall in love with yourself. Know that you are loveable.

Big love is possible for anyone, of any age, if you are willing to become a magnet for love. Continue to live each day in the knowingness that you are in a loving, committed relationship as you savor the waiting for your beloved to arrive.

Arielle Ford has spent the past 20 years living and promoting consciousness through all forms of media. She is the author of six books including the *HOT CHOCOLATE FOR THE MYSTICAL SOUL* series. Her next book, *THE SOULMATE SECRET: The Law of Attraction for Love* will be published January 2009. She lives in La Jolla, CA with her husband.

Please visit her websites www.EverythingYouShouldKnow.com, www.FordSisters.com and www.SoulmateKit.com.

Build Loyalty and Your Business Will Succeed

Heide & Christian Holtz

What an absolute incredible journey we've been on. We've spent the past 5 years building our various online businesses, Hurraz.com, one of the most successful loyalty reward programs on the web, My RevenuePlace.com, our career center for online jobs and income opportunities, Ad-Synergy.com our own advertising agency serving millions of ads a month, and SmarterSites.net our favorite product, a successful money-making-website.

How We Got Started

Back in 2002, Christian, my then 17 year old son and I hardly had any time to see each other. I had a demanding corporate job that was killing me. I was working from 8:00 am to 10.00 pm, 7 days a week, and my life was all about getting our bills paid and credit ratings! Nothing we had or owned seemed to make us happy. I knew then it was time to make a 180 degree change. I wrote down on paper how my ideal day should be: I wanted to get up in the morning; have breakfast with my son; go to the gym; work until lunch time; go sailing; work another couple of hours; meet up with friends for coffee; view the sunset from the deck of my luxurious home… and travel anytime I want.

There was quite a contrast between my life back then and how I really wanted us to spend our days. Action was required, but how?

Christian and I had already been trying to make money through the internet for some time. We looked at hundreds of companies, and actually signed up with a number of them, but we didn't make any money. It seemed as though most companies only wanted our investment capital: they either required an upfront investment before we could even find out what the business was about or that we spend money to make money. Others required a certain sales quota to qualify for payment and they didn't even roll over the commissions into the next month. One company simply didn't pay anyone and at least they got shut down quickly. The overall feeling we got from our experience is that none of these companies were designed for the new affiliates to succeed and they all had one thing in common: only a few people at the top were earning money.

Something had to change!

This time we were working on a "contrast list" about income opportunities. On the left we wrote down all that was lacking or wrong with each of the companies we looked at or worked for, and on the right how we thought it should be.

We had found our mission!

We were starting a new online business that would make sense to everyone involved. It had to be easy to understand, easy to make money and include all the necessary web promotion and monetization tools. We knew that if it made sense for the new affiliates and the end user, we would be successful.

How exciting!

What could be more rewarding than to achieve our goals, our financial freedom while helping others do the same! We knew it wouldn't be easy, but the rewards would be life changing, and so it was!

The Journey

Within only 2 years of starting our first online business, we had built one of the most successful reward programs on the web, providing at that time an extra income to 7,000 members around the world. We succeeded over tens of thousands of other online businesses out there and for one reason only - we stayed true to the philosophy that we still maintain today: "Build loyalty and your business will succeed."

What you need to know!

We didn't have any experience with programmers, or scripts or how to edit a website, much less hosting companies, marketing or advertising. It wasn't easy. We made all the mistakes in the book and then some, but we persevered.

Each mistake was a lesson learned and a step closer to success!

With all the accumulated experience and after the tremendous success with our first program, we were now empowered and inspired to teach others how to succeed on the internet. We created three new companies to do just that. First came our online career center to assist people in finding the right online job or income opportunity. Then about a year after that, we founded our ad agency, and in 2007 we launched our favorite product SmarterSites.net, to assist regular internet users in starting their own money making e-business FAST.

What a blast!

The more we were helping others, the more money we were all making. We had created a worldwide community of like-minded people that understood the value of loyalty and sharing success, therefore we all benefited from each other.

You too, will succeed. You just need to allow it!

Too many times we've seen wonderful people with great ideas. They believe in them, but then for some reason, they don't seem to think they deserve to succeed. It is so much easier to find reasons why NOT to succeed, so they end up blocking everything good they had coming to them.

You don't need to be a genius or have any previous experience to succeed. The Law of Attraction says like attracts like; good creates more good; success creates more success.

You will be among friends on your journey to achieve your goals!

Christian and I love every minute of our days as we spend our time helping others to achieve financial freedom.

What a joy that is!

Will you be the next? Just imagine how your life could be earning an extra $3,000 to $10,000 a month, working only a couple of hours a day!

Just give yourself the chance to experience true freedom!

Your life will be filled with new experiences, opportunities and possibilities. You will have the time to do the things you love, with the people you love and plenty of money pouring in from all directions – guaranteed!

Life can be truly amazing!

Financial freedom gives you wings. You can achieve anything you want, no matter where you are or what your current situation is. Just remember, always stay true to your mission, allow yourself to succeed and you will experience prosperity and abundance in all areas of your life FAST!

Tip # 1: Make your own "Contrast list." On the left of a page write down all the things you are not happy with in your life, and on the right how your ideal day should be. See on paper what areas need to change in your life and take the necessary action!

Tip # 2: Allow yourself to achieve financial freedom. Everything you desire is already out there waiting for you! Focus on what you desire (positive vibration) and not so much on your doubts (negative vibration). Doubt is created by limiting beliefs. Believe in your dreams and let the "Law of Attraction" work for you.

Tip # 3: Joining us can be YOUR ADVANTAGE to achieve your goals. You will be among friends on your journey to prosperity and success, a worldwide community of like-minded entrepreneurs willing to share our success with you. Experience the power of positive vibration pouring straight into your life.

Tip # 4: Build Loyalty and your business will succeed! Always stay true to your mission. While most businesses spend millions of dollars on advertising, through loyalty we can help you build a system that is far more successful and without the expense!

Heide Holtz, founder of LoyaltePAYS Corporation & Ad-Synergy.com and Christian Holtz, Masters of Business Finance, awarded 1ˢᵗ prize for Successful Entrepreneur at Bond University, Australia in 2007 and director of MyRevenuePlace.com and SmarterSites.net, derive great satisfaction for providing already a better income to thousands of internet users worldwide. Joining us can be YOUR advantage to financial freedom. Go to http://loyaltepays.com, sign-up for the newsletter in the referrer field, enter the word **Loyalty** and receive 2 excellent money making tools!

NOT ONLY SURVIVED, BUT THRIVED!
- A SPIRITED JOURNEY

Teresa Finocchiaro

The date was 4th July, 2004. That was the day I told my husband that I wanted to leave our 25 year marriage. It was the most terrifying experience of my life. At the end of our conversation, I was on the floor curled up in a fetal position, heart palpitating, my body convulsing.

It was not a decision I made lightly. I deliberated about it for two years. During that time I agonized over how it would affect our two beautiful teenaged children. I felt guilty because I had made a solemn vow, in church, that we would remain married until we were parted by death, and I had taken that vow very seriously. I also knew that staying in the marriage was detrimental to my soul and well-being. I had suffered deep depression and was desperately unhappy. My soul's imperative urging was difficult to ignore any longer and I had to dig deep within myself and find the courage to do what I had to do.

Gut-wrenching fear paralyzed me as I faced a life without money or a home, as my husband wanted to keep the house. I had married at age 19, going from my parents' home directly to my husband's home. Having never lived independently and never been solely responsible for paying my bills, the prospect of moving out of our home terrified me. Such was my fear that I stayed in the family home, living in the guest bedroom for two years before I took the plunge and moved out.

In my 20's and 30's I had very low self-esteem and very little confidence in myself. I started to read self-help and personal development books and continued to devour them one by one for 15 years. These books and my training in Transformational Breathwork,

Life Coaching and Reiki, had taken me to the stage where I had the strength to even conceive of making such a monumental decision.

However, deep down I still had the limiting belief that I did not know enough and felt like a fraud. I did not encourage my practice to grow, even though my clients were experiencing amazing breakthroughs in their lives and were extremely grateful for my facilitating their journeys to wholeness and authenticity, and telling me what I gifted healer I was.

I realized that I needed a reliable, steady income, so I made the decision to get a job. I had been trained and worked as a Personal Assistant (PA) in my 20's, then left full-time corporate work once I had my children. My challenge was that I had not worked as a PA for many years and felt like a technological dinosaur. I was distraught at the thought that no-one would employ me, so my confidence levels plummeted. Updating my computer skills was not going to be enough after such a long absence from the workplace. Fortunately, a good friend of mine, a director in a stock-broking firm, gave me the opportunity to improve my skills and boost my confidence when his PA moved on to another position. It was only a temporary position for two months; however it was enough of a stepping stone to get back into the working game again.

It was time to take stock. I taught my clients about the Law of Attraction and that our thoughts are creative. Here was the perfect opportunity for me to fully practice what I preached.

Every night I wrote ten things in my gratitude journal that I was grateful for. It helped me to focus on what was wonderful in my life instead of what was not. I continually focused on the abundance all around me. I also wrote out a vision for myself - of what I wanted to create in all areas of my life, such as living in a lovely home in a desirable neighborhood, multiple streams of income, time to spend in Italy reconnecting with my roots, developing my healing practice and related products, writing a book, and having a beautiful relationship with a life partner.

Manifesting took unwavering faith and belief in myself - in my personal power. I also had to remove the mental blockages and limiting beliefs that were impeding my process and sabotaging my efforts.

So it began.

In 2005 I attracted to myself what I thought was a real estate investment mentoring program which turned out to be so much more. I had no money to fund this program, yet I just knew in my soul that I needed to do it. A way was found. I remembered that I had an old paid up life insurance policy that had accumulated some benefits over the years, so I took the money I needed for the course from there. After I joined the program, the participants were informed that there would be a competition, where we would write about where we were at financially and why we wanted to do this program. Ten of us would have the opportunity to receive the program for free, as well as receive personal mentoring throughout the program. To my absolute amazement, I was chosen as one of the ten. Thank you, Universe!

Some of the major things I have since manifested are:

- A 12 month contract as an Office Manager, which was the perfect length of time to suit my needs.

- A lovely, spacious, apartment for myself and my daughter, in a beautiful affluent area, suiting all our needs and for a rent that was under market value.

- A trip to Europe for 8 weeks to reconnect with my Italian roots.

- The most wonderful life partner with whom I have a deep soul connection.

- A magnificent home where 5 years earlier I had expressed a desire to buy a property. The Universe never forgets an order!

- Putting into practice what I learned in the mentoring program, I bought two high quality investment properties within 4 months of each other. They have literally fallen into my lap!

- Clients who are serious about healing and transforming their lives.

Life just keeps getting better every day as I continue to attract my unlimited desires to myself. So far in 2008, I have manifested being a published author and another trip to Europe. On my European trip in 2007, I expressed my desire to my family and friends to return in April. I didn't give it much thought once I had returned home. I have since received an invitation to attend a wedding in Europe on March 30th, 2008, thus giving me the nudge to make solid plans to go. Once again, the Universe delivered!

My life has been totally transformed. I now walk my walk with conviction and it is my joy and passion to work with clients as a life healer and transformation specialist. I am humbled and in awe as I witness my clients reconnect with their spirit, feel light and free, with increased aliveness and vitality. It is a very rejuvenating experience, their lives totally transformed.

I want you to *know*, and *believe* the absolute truth of who you are: that you are an *unlimited* being, with *unlimited* power.

With immense love and compassion for people, **Teresa Finocchiaro** is a highly intuitive, gifted, life transformation specialist. Her skill lies in her innate ability to accurately pinpoint the underlying issues that her clients have. Through individual consultations, courses and workshops, Teresa guides her clients on a fascinating journey through their inner space. For more information and free resources, visit www.SpiritedJourneys.com or to contact Teresa directly, email her at Teresa@SpiritedJourneys.com.

The Butterfly Message

Suzanne Schwartz

Welcome! I, the Butterfly, am the Beloved's companion and you are the Beloved. I have been assigned a divine mission. It is to inspire and encourage you in nurturing your spiritual capacity as the Beloved.

This is "it", the Butterfly Message. Yet, I suspect that just like mine once was, your response is "Who cares? What's this got to do with me?"

So I continue to tell my story and explain how it was in the school of hard knocks that I came to an understanding of what it was telling me. But first, a little bit of background to put you in the picture.

I was born on the African continent, in a country that is now called Zimbabwe. My childhood years were spent growing up on a beautiful ranch which my parents had chosen to make their home and raise their family. It was situated in the southern part of the country called Matabeleland. The people who live in the Fort Rixon district where my parents' farm was located, are from the Ndebele tribe and their language is called Ndebele. They are an offshoot of the Zulu tribe whose home is in the KwaZulu – Natal province of South Africa.

"Ivevane" is a word in the Ndebele language which means "Butterfly." I had no idea how significant this word would become in my life. To me, it was merely a name given to the spinning and weaving enterprise that my Mother had set up on the farm. It seemed an appropriate enough name, given the circumstances in which it was her intention to help school drop outs whose parents had lived and worked on the farm for many years. The chances of these young people finding employment were almost non-existent and there was not much in their future to look forward to, except days of boredom and getting into trouble.

She felt she could bring about a change for the better by offering to teach anyone willing to acquire a new skill, how to spin and weave. It was decided to call the group that took up her offer "Ivevane" meaning "Butterfly." It wasn't long before they were turning the cotton waste that my mother was able to obtain at low cost from a factory, into a variety of hand crafted, woven products ranging from rugs to cushions. These sold well at fairs, craft markets and by word of mouth, and the profits that accrued were shared among members of the group. For a number of years, "Ivevane" grew from strength to strength, until one of its members, the only man in the group, was the person who killed my mother.

It was in December 1993, that I received the news that she had been brutally assaulted by this man in her home on the farm. For 10 days she lay in a coma in an intensive care unit before dying as a result of severe head injuries sustained in the attack.

With the way it happened so suddenly, I felt betrayed, abandoned and very alone. Yet, in the midst of all the chaos and upheaval caused by this event, I could not help but notice a series of coincidences, linked in one way or another to my Mother's death. Their common thread was the Butterfly. The first one to draw my attention was "Ivevane" or "Butterfly", the name she had given to her weaving enterprise. It came to mean more than just a word to me especially when coincidences in other areas of my life simultaneously began to reveal the Butterfly.

I sensed there was more to these happenings than met the eye, but didn't know what exactly. So, I went looking for answers in books on spirituality and metaphysics. While they provided me with some insights, there was nothing that seemed to fully "explain" the incredible coincidences I was experiencing with the Butterfly in my *own* life.

Not knowing where to turn next, I began documenting their details, mainly so that I would remember them. The steps I took to write them down helped me realize that contained in each coincidence was an encrypted message that I could decode through a process of introspection.

In hindsight, I realize that without the occurrence of these butterfly coincidences and then taking some action to write them down, I dread to think what would have become of me. Their combination inspired me with a new lease of life and focus. If you find yourself in a similar situation, my advice is to describe in words and pictures, if necessary, how you really think and feel about it. Let it come from your heart and not only your head. While you are doing this, also pay attention to any coincidences or synchronicity that may be going on around you. It could lead to new insights and fresh perspectives that might not have become apparent otherwise. Even if you find that's not always the case, you'll feel a whole lot lighter by putting it in writing and getting it off your chest.

In 1999, I relocated with my husband and two children from Zimbabwe to live in Perth, Western Australia. To my amazement, I continued to experience coincidences with the Butterfly. While we set about the daunting process of starting our lives from scratch, it meant so much and was very reassuring to know that it was around and still there for me as the Beloved's companion.

All the coincidences I have experienced have produced numerous Butterfly messages, although they are really variations of the one theme. Namely, the Butterfly is the Beloved's companion and as a member of the human race, I am one of its billions of Beloveds. Once I got "it" and understood this about myself and the Butterfly's role in my life, I felt empowered to collect all the Butterfly messages I had deciphered over the years into the kind of book I wished had been around when I had experienced the devastating loss of my mother.

While the Butterfly Message has brought me comfort, healing and teaching, it has also become my passion, purpose and calling. I feel compelled and propelled to share it with you, for it is my hope that it will inspire you to see yourself in a new light and start you on your own journey as the Beloved. I believe that when more people are able to fall in love with themselves, it helps to make this world a better place. The Butterfly Message is my way of reaching out to all, though especially women, who live on this planet today in a spirit of love and a bond of common humanity. Heaven knows this planet is desperate for more love and what better place to start than with ourselves.

Suzanne is a mother of two nearly grown up children and a teacher working with teen refugees in an Intensive English Centre. She aims to live a life that is reflective of the truth of her being which is love for herself and others. She has designed a set of Butterfly Message cards for this purpose.

Visit www.TheButterflyMessage.com to receive a free set of Butterfly Message cards plus hints and ways to use them.

How NLP can Change Your Way of Thinking

Yvonne Goold

Over many years of reading books and participating in personal development courses, I've come to realize that what is manifested in our physical universe is the external results of our internal thinking, whether mental, emotional or spiritual. As a result, I feel very blessed with my present life: I have a gorgeous supportive husband, my own business and am very happy with the way things are. But it didn't all come together overnight. This is how I made my dreams happen.

I've always been very curious about how things work – why is it so? What would happen if I tried this or that? What's it all about? This curiosity has provided me with the drive and incentive to look at my life and surroundings from various angles. As many have done, I've looked at different aspects of myself and noticed some things I didn't like and wanted to change, and other things I wanted to develop or improve.

A turning point in my life came one day when I noticed a man standing on a city sidewalk with a clipboard. He seemed out of place and lost in his own world. As I'd never seen anyone with a clipboard on the sidewalk before, I asked him what he was doing. This appeared to startle him. I agreed to participate in the questionnaire he was conducting, and as a result of the analysis of my answers, my perspective about myself was substantially altered and I became aware of some characteristics which could be improved. I bought a personal development book and started to read it as soon as I got home.

During the previous months I had begun to change things in my life that I wasn't happy with, like having a 6-month break from consuming any alcohol. My reasoning at the time was, "Let's see if I can go without alcohol for 6 months, as a trial." I included "as a trial" in case I wanted to go back to what I was doing without feeling guilty about it. After I made the decision to stop, I found it easy to abstain from alcohol and had no desire to resume my old habits at the end of the trial. In fact, the combination of no alcohol affecting my thoughts or actions, along with new concepts from the personal development book I had bought, and becoming more aware of myself and what I wanted to do, enabled me to gain a new clarity of direction. I moved out of the house I was living in and signed up for evening classes in mathematics. The next major change was to become a non-smoker. All of these changes were just the start of my personal development journey which has been continuing for about 20 years now.

Each step led to new challenges, and the next one I decided to undertake was to study at University. This proved more demanding than the technical college I'd previously attended and I struggled. It was around this time I was introduced to kinesiology which helped release the stress, negative emotions and other imbalances I was experiencing. Because I'd gained so much from the kinesiology, I decided to learn it after completing university.

I have written down, visualized and manifested many dreams & goals into my reality.

One of my dreams was to have my own business, but this appeared to be elusive. Deciding what business to be in has taken me many years while working in different industries in a variety of roles, some of which I thoroughly enjoyed and some, not so much. This variety has enabled me to gain many perspectives and valuable experiences, all building on each other.

Then I came across NLP (Neuro-Linguistic Programming) which addresses how we hear, feel or see our reality, and how we react or respond to situations via visual, auditory or kinesthetic means. NLP can be used by anyone who wants to change something about their life. Like getting to your ideal weight, becoming a non-smoker, changing bad or nervous habits like nail biting, eliminating a fear of heights, flying, or speaking etc., or even controlling irrational or volatile behavior such as road rage. NLP is all about changing disempowering experiences into empowering ones by asking questions in such a way that causes the individual to create new neurological pathways and arrive at the "aha" moment. Different techniques are used for different issues. They could involve visualizations which use visual, auditory and/or kinesthetic senses to release negative experiences or to reinforce positive emotions, resulting in permanent empowering changes. Whatever you'd like to change about yourself, NLP techniques can unlock your own inner potential and hand you the controls.

I have had some amazing shifts in behaviors and thinking using NLP techniques. From "couldn't be bothered exercising" to actually looking for ways to exercise each day, to obliterating negative emotions and moving out of "feeling stuck." I've also reduced my consumption of chocolates and sweets, so that I am in control of what I eat and there's no feeling of being deprived.

I LOVE seeing the positive changes and amazing transformations in those I have coached. This involves a change in their own thinking which results in a change in their external results towards what they want to achieve. My belief gets reinforced each time I see that what is manifested in our physical universe is the external results of our internal thinking, whether mental, emotional or spiritual.

Looking back, it may have taken me longer to accomplish these things had I not taken that first step of stopping the alcohol that was clouding my thinking, although I didn't realize it at the time. Becoming a non-smoker has resulted in better connections with others and an increased sensitivity to smells. Reading so many personal development books has opened up many areas in my life for me to reflect on, and has led me to where I am today.

My personal growth is ongoing, as is listening/watching personal development CD's, DVD's, and participating in other programs which assist me in some way to be more of the me I want to be. I do this because it reinforces positive principles and helps me realize that there's always another perspective to situations, and I tend to learn something else when listening/watching the CD/DVD again. Another thing I've noticed is that if something isn't working the way I want, the best thing to do is find out what's going on internally first, then look at external factors.

As the saying goes, "If you're not growing, you're dying."

An exercise for you: Notice how you're feeling, what's going on physically, mentally, emotionally, spiritually. Put that aside for now and recall a time that you felt *really alive* - you were bursting with energy, maybe even overflowing with it. Really *feel* the feelings of being totally alive; *hear* what you heard, *see* what you saw, recall the feeling of *bursting with energy*, being *right* there... and smile. As you're feeling, hearing and seeing this sensation, touch one of your knuckles while the feeling/sensations are strong, and let go before the feeling/sensations subside. Repeat a few times with other experiences when you felt *really alive*. If you're feeling a bit low sometime, press the same knuckle – you'll probably end up smiling and feeling the same feelings/sensations of being *totally alive*.

Yvonne assists clients to gain clarity of direction in their lives. With over 2 decades of experience working in a variety of industries and an engineering degree, she is now a full-time personal coach. Yvonne loves to see positive changes happen in her client's lives as they easily adjust their internal thinking to achieve the results they desire.

Contact Yvonne via <u>Coaching@ProvenStrategies.com.au</u> or visit <u>www.ProvenStrategies.com.au/FreeAudio.html</u> to find out how to easily release a negative emotion.

LEAP OF FAITH

Margot Wiburd

"Sound!"

"Camera!"

"Action!"

I had it all. I worked in Australia as the personal assistant to a charismatic, internationally acclaimed film director. I mixed with actors, writers and musicians.

I'd travelled widely and enjoyed colorful careers in advertising, television, teaching English as a Second Language and jewelry design, but now a small voice hovered, insistent, in my mind. It forced me to admit that, despite the outer glitz of my life, inside I felt like a non-event. Unoriginal. Empty.

Only one thing could fill this constant void: the sight of a beautiful painting. It could make me catch my breath...cause the entire world to drop away in an instant.

I harbored a secret ambition. I wanted to change my life. I wanted to learn to paint – not as a hobby, but seriously. I wanted to follow a creative calling that would challenge and stretch my inner resources to the limit, show what I was capable of. And I wanted to be independent - dance to my own tune.

I looked in the mirror. "Reality check! You're 42, you've never saved a penny in your life and you expect to start again after *how* many careers?" Surely we have only so many chances in life? Wasn't I too old? Could I risk all for the romantic notion of becoming an artist?

Dreams are essential, but they require foundations. I did my research. An art magazine ran an ad for a two-week painting course at the highly regarded Academy of Realist Art in Seattle. If only I could afford the fee. A small line of print caught my eye. "Limited scholarships available."

I hastily took snapshots of my tiny collection of drawings and sent them to the school's director, together with a sincere letter detailing my request.

A week later, a handwritten fax arrived. "Congratulations! Margot, we can offer you the scholarship for our "Intro to Oil Painting Workshop." Amazing what happens when you ask.

My employer wasn't grumpy about my impending absence. Actually he was proud of me for broadening my horizons. "I'll pay for your airfare," he said, clinching the deal. It's interesting how creatively satisfied people seem to celebrate other people's successes, while those who never dare to step outside their comfort zones are the first to raise objections.

In Seattle I went from being a clumsy ignoramus to acquiring basic skills in painting, and the experience focused my dreams. In that short space of time I learned enough to create a small folio of artwork. I learned, too, of a private art school in the Loire Valley in France. The momentum was building.

L'Ecole Albert de Fois offered six months intense tuition in classical oil painting. I could follow this with 6 months at a school in New York, if I felt it necessary. But I needed money - a lot! $28,000 if I was going to study for a year.

I've always believed in the good of people and hoped that somewhere, someone might understand my vision. With nothing to lose and everything to gain, I decided to create my own sponsorship campaign.

Combing the telephone books, I carefully selected companies, creative luminaries and prominent citizens - anyone who appeared to have money, leadership or vision. I wrote, revised and rewrote what I would say, laying my heart bare in personalized letters to over 200 individuals. I described my intense passion, clearly outlined the practical steps I would take to achieve my dream and asked for financial assistance in any amount. My friends applauded my optimism. An accountant scoffed, "No one will give you money for nothing." "You might be right," I replied, "but how will I know if I don't try?" His skepticism strengthened my resolve.

The rejection letters trickled, then flooded in. I had not imagined there were so many ways for people to say no. Soon I began to dread the postman's knock. Heart in hand I waited while the days crawled by.

Then one morning a message on the answering machine brought goose bumps to my skin. "Margot, I received your letter. I empathize with what you want to do and I'd love to do the same, but I have a small child, and a business to run. I can't give you all the money you need…but I can give you $10,000."

A week later, my benefactor – a confident, radiant heiress with much imagination and an even bigger heart - presented me with a check for $10,000. It was sufficient to cover six months tuition in France. I was away to the land of *café au lait* and fresh, flaky croissants!

In the beginning, it was paradise.

Then my dream turned to torment.

Each day brought fresh humiliation in front of the other, more talented students. I'd thought I'd be brilliant at what I wanted so much. Now it seemed I had to work twice as hard as the others just to keep up. My colleagues looked at me with pity. I loved what I was trying to do, but it just wasn't coming together.

In an effort to counter my feelings of failure, I studied French in my free time. Every evening under a canopy of stars I walked the quiet country roads, repeating the words from my cassette player.

I am happy. *Je suis heureuse.*

I am afraid. *J'ai peur.*

I noticed how each time I repeated a downbeat phrase such as, "I am sad," I felt instantly heavy and leaden. Happy, positive phrases put a spring in my step. I was experiencing the power of affirmations.

Back in the classroom, my lack of genius continued. My course would soon be over and after months of persistence and effort, I felt defeated and useless. One cold, foggy night, feeling utterly desperate, my feet pounded the roadside as I tried to walk off some of my frustration. Beside myself with emotion, I stopped and from the depths of my soul sent a raw plea to the heavens. "I don't understand. What's wrong with me? Should I just give up? I want this with all my heart. Please! Give. Me. A. Sign."

Next day began as usual. Then…everything changed.

Pigment flowed effortlessly, flawlessly, from my brush. Stroke after stroke, my work glowed, subtle…inviting…*beautiful*! It was as though I were wrapped in an invisible cloak of perfection, another, eminently skilled hand guiding my brush.

My teacher went to stroll past, then stopped cold. Staring over my shoulder for what seemed an eternity, he suddenly announced. "Everyone, gather around. This is how it's done."

Was it some kind of divine intervention? Was it mind over matter, where the power of thought can influence, even change, one's future? Or had the constant flow of technical information simply crystallized in one dramatic moment? Whatever the reason, something inside had shifted. For the first time, I felt whole. I no longer needed to look outside myself for happiness; I possessed a source of joy from *within*. A singular, lasting talent that was my very own.

Not long ago I sipped champagne in a vast overseas gallery. The walls overflowed with shimmering pastel drawings and oil paintings by the chosen Artist in Residence. It was an uplifting, glorious sight. It was also my 50th birthday - and I was that artist.

Margot Wiburd lives in beautiful Mandurah in Western Australia, where she works as an artist, writer and film crewmember. She is finalizing a memoir of her intriguing life in film and art, a documentary on her overseas artist residency and a book to assist upcoming artists. Visit www.MargotWiburd.com to receive *Almost an Artist* – great advice for creative souls, and take a peek at Margot's art. You can also contact her at Margotaw@netspace.net.au.

Do What You Love and Prosper

Brigitte Smith

Working as a professional (a lawyer), earning a reasonable income, and with some knowledge of investing, you might be excused for thinking I was doing reasonably well. Yet as a single parent with two teenaged children and a limited prosperity consciousness, I was pretty much standing still from a financial point of view. I could see that I needed to diversify if I was to achieve true financial freedom for myself and my boys.

So in the little spare time that I had, I started working on developing my prosperity consciousness by reading a mountain of self-help books and joining a "wealth creating" master mind group. My journey had begun.

And on the practical side, I started looking at developing an income online.

But where would I start?

Always having been an advocate of holistic health, at around this time I started to realize that many of the people I knew followed a healthy lifestyle for themselves by making conscious food choices and avoiding traditional medicine when there were more natural alternatives available.

Like many people (currently over 50 percent of households in developed nations), I'm a pet owner. I have two dogs, a Rottweiler, Kara, and a Staffordshire Bull Terrier, Jet. They're both coming up to 13 years old, and are very much part of our family. Our dogs are really pretty spoiled, and have come to believe that their place is in the house, and as a consequence, can become quite indignant when they're told to go outside!

Pets bring real joy to many people. The fact that dogs (and cats) are now being used in aged care facilities, nursing homes, hospices and children's hospitals attest to this fact. The very presence of these animals has been shown to hasten recovery and otherwise bring an atmosphere of calmness and wellbeing to residents and patients.

Dogs, in particular, are incredibly loyal to their owners. They rarely complain about anything, are happy just to be fed and given a little attention, and are invariably ecstatic to see their owners come home even if they've only been gone for 10 minutes! Such unconditional affection is rarely seen in people.

Their loyalty ensures that dogs, appropriately trained, are excellent as assistance animals for the disabled. The origins of guide dogs for the blind are somewhat obscure as dogs seem to have been used in this capacity in various cultures, for a very long time. Seeing eye dogs in the form we know them today have been around since at least the 1920's. And today, guide dogs are trained for people with various types of disabilities, giving many people a greater quality of life than they would enjoy without these assistance dogs.

And for all the joy they bring, dogs ask in return only that we feed them, keep them clean and free from disease.

I'd read that one should build a business around something one is passionate about, so I decided to try my hand at educating pet owners about different points of view relating to pet health. I also wanted to ensure that my dogs enjoy a healthy and long life into the bargain.

I subscribed to one of those "Do-it-yourself" type website builders four years back, and started developing my website, HealthyHappyDogs.com. I wrote a free report on basic dog health (that I've rewritten several times since then), and gave it away on my site.

Writing about my own experiences as a dog owner, and pointing readers to products and materials that they might find helpful in their quest to keep their pets in great health, became my part-time mission. I somehow fit this new venture in between my prosperity consciousness building, my professional life and my family life with all that that entails with two, at times, rather rebellious teenage boys.

Progress was slow at first, because attracting people to one's website is not just a matter of throwing up a site and hoping people will come. An online business is quite different to a bricks and mortar business in this regard.

However, over the past four years, I've built several sites about pets (and other topics), and discovered how best to bring people to those sites. The most recent addition to my pet sites is my HealthierDogs. com site. Subscribers to my Healthy Happy Dogs online newsletter now number over eleven thousand. I've managed to extend my reach to thousands of pet owners by a combination of expanding my prosperity consciousness and plain old-fashioned hard work. And I've only just skimmed the tip of the iceberg. As I said, there are millions of pet owners out there, so even if I expand exponentially by a factor of ten each year for the next two or three years, I will still only be scratching the surface.

Achieving this exponential growth will at some stage include a paid membership site, where other like-minded pet owners can come together and more effectively spread the word that our pets really do deserve better. Our pets deserve at the very least, for their owners to be informed of the true facts concerning pet health, rather than the distorted facts peddled by solely profit-driven commercial pet food manufacturers and veterinary pharmaceutical companies.

Not being confined by a physical location, the beauty of an online business is that it can be international in scope. Mine is. Although the majority of my readers reside in the United States, I also have readers in Canada, the United Kingdom, France, Germany, Australia, New Zealand, the Philippines, Singapore, South Africa, India, and many more. Being able to make an impact on dog owners, and their dogs' lives, around the world really feels like a great accomplishment. And the feedback I get from readers of my sites is a real-time indicator of just how well my business is going.

Freedom – that's what I started this business for. And bit by bit, I'm achieving that freedom, be it in the form of overseas travel that I may otherwise not have indulged in, and extra time – that has to be the best benefit of all. Although initially, and up until now, I've been putting every minute of time that I have available into building my business, that is now starting to change. Some of the promotional work for my sites is now outsourced, and that outsourcing will grow. Consequently, I'm going to have more and more time to do whatever I want. Perhaps I'll put a lot of that time back into the dogs. Perhaps I'll start a new venture. And perhaps I'll just relax and take life easy!

To be able to inform pet owners of alternatives to conventional diet, drugs and chemicals, and to be developing an ever-growing income as a wonderful consequence of that, is a dream come true.

Brigitte Smith is a self confessed 'dogaholic' with a passion for improving the health of our pets. Brigitte's vision is to reverse the trend of pets living shortened lives due to poor nutrition and overuse of chemicals and drugs. Her free report *How to Improve Your Dog's Health Within 30 Days and Maybe Even Lengthen Your Dog's Life* is available at http://www.HealthyHappyDogs.com and you can catch up on what else Brigitte is up to at http://www.BrigitteSmith.com.

Blindfolded Beginner to Millionaire Manifestor

Annette Thomas

My journey from blindfolded beginner to millionaire manifestor began at the age of 25. I wrote a goal to be worth $5M, have two children and be living in my home overlooking the ocean. That seemingly unrealistic dream at the time materialized exactly 10 years later.

Sounds great, doesn't it? It wasn't all 'go with the flow' – quite the opposite. I believe that challenges happen in our life for a reason, often to test us to see how much we truly want something, and to help us become the person we are required to be so that we can have what we desire.

My Mum always told me that to be successful in life you have to do the opposite of everyone else that life is about taking risks. I would not be in the position I am today, if the person I had always dreamed of being hadn't gotten a few things wrong some of the time. Often it is just one thing that tips the scales of success on your side. However, you don't know what that thing is when you are taking the risk. That's why it appears as an unknown variable.

After reading 'Unlimited Power' by Tony Robbins, I was immediately inspired to take further action to bring my dream into reality by reading as many books on personal development as possible. I was motivated by the fact his goal was to live in a house overlooking the ocean with his family. I too wanted the sports car, excellent health, beautiful family and money, and if he could have it, so could I. I visualized myself with all those things and felt really good about it. The truth is I didn't really believe it was possible at the time, I just wished it was. My husband and I had a large mortgage on our suburban home, less than average incomes and no great ideas.

I boldly approached my husband and announced, "Guess what! I want to be worth $5M and be living in a home overlooking the ocean!" I was so excited by stating this fact. My euphoria lasted about 10 seconds as the reply from him was "Don't be ridiculous! What are you trying to do to me?" He was experiencing tightness in his chest and I thought he was going to have a heart attack! Great! I walked away, feeling rejected, and angry from his lack of support, but knew I would just have to find a way and perhaps be a little less vocal about my dream.

At the time I didn't know how it was going to happen, but I decided to research investment options, go to mainly free seminars, listen to tapes and read as many books as possible. I realized that you cannot solve a problem with the same mindset in which it was created.

I had a love/hate relationship with money. While I struggled to save money to buy curtains, get a concrete driveway and landscaping for our home, I didn't give myself permission to spend too much money furthering my personal development. My self-esteem was not where it could be, and I didn't value myself highly enough. My dream was in trouble of remaining just that - a dream. With a husband who hated change, I was challenged to move forward.

Shortly after declaring my goal, I had a car accident that very nearly cost me my life, which in hindsight was a huge wake up call that I just wasn't ready to listen to. I received a small payout through insurance, which allowed me to afford a 5% deposit on a new housing unit in Sydney's western suburbs and to dabble in the stock market. The stock market experience was a shocker and I wasted almost $12,000, which was a huge amount to me at that time. The housing unit, unbeknown to us at the time, became the first rung on the ladder to building a successful property portfolio. I have since been involved in two other share-trading systems, both of which have not performed to my expectations, and I have had to take losses and move on. From these two experiences, I have learned that I would be better putting more energy into the type of investing I love, namely property.

We played the game well and played it hard. We leveraged our home and first investment property at a time when the market was booming, and rode the wave of success to own 24 properties in 5 years. It was challenging, scary, fun and empowering all at the same time.

The lessons I learned about responsibility were many layered. The first level - go to work, earn money, have integrity, be a good partner etc., then on another level – that I alone was responsible for improving my life and no-one else. The buck stopped with me. It was my understanding of the Law of Attraction that taught me the next level of responsibility – that we create everything in our lives. Wow, talk about a paradigm shift!

After 'The Secret' was released, I became even more ferociously curious about the Law of Attraction and how to live the dream life I had always envisioned for myself. I watched the DVD more than 10 times, bought and gave away 20 copies to friends and family, and tried to absorb the concept and put it into practice.

The challenging part was that while I understood the Law of Attraction intellectually, the results weren't showing up in my life. Now if you are thinking, "This girl should be happy", you are right. I am happy! Very. I have achieved a lot and I call myself ambitious and wear it like a badge. I am also very grateful. No matter what we achieve in life, we will always want more. That doesn't mean I am not satisfied, it just means I am moving to the 'next level of the game.' I now have learned that happiness can truly only come from within. It doesn't come when I achieve a goal, make money, or someone gives me a compliment. While those things are really great experiences, I know that I decide whether to be happy despite what happens to me in my life.

Since discovering the manifestation process, I have achieved a spiritual breakthrough I had longed for, a beautiful level of inner peace, and a dramatically heightened level of intuition. Other manifestations include new inspiring friends, owning a business I am passionate about, improving my child's chronic infections, and meeting my dream partner after separating from my husband. Smaller wants such as car parking spaces and finding lost items are part of my day-to-day enjoyment of manifesting.

I like to keep my personal process of manifesting simple, and I'm sharing it with you. Here it is: know what you want, ask (the Universe, God, your religion) for it, in a relaxed and confident state. Feel the feelings of experiencing it as if you have it now, feel grateful... and then let it go. The results you achieve can be hindered by constantly negative thought processes, being attached to the outcome or concentrating too strongly on the 'how.' Yes, it really is that simple.

Annette Thomas' contribution to this book is a manifestation of her lifelong dream to become a writer who helps others achieve a more fulfilling life experience. She is a 36 year old, successful property investor, author, world traveler, and mother of 2, living in a beautiful home overlooking the ocean in Coffs Harbour, Australia. Visit her website www.ManifestYourFutureNow.com for a free e-book on self-improvement tips and further information on how to bring your dreams to reality.

What a Truly Empowering and Magnificent Gift Cancer Has Been to Me

Gaia Sharne Singer

One day it wasn't there – two days later, it was – a 2.5 cm lump on my left breast near my armpit, and so close to the surface that it was easily seen. "Goodness!" was my first thought, "Where the heck did that come from?"

Did I feel any fear? No. I was purely curious as to how such a large lump could have appeared literally within 48 hours. "Oh well," I thought, "it must be a cyst." Mum had suffered really badly with them.

I remembered that in my 30's I had come across a small lump in my left breast and had nearly gone crazy with fear. I had always had a great fear of losing a breast and often would ask my husband (long since my ex) whether he would still find me desirable if this happened. He would always laugh, but never gave me a clear reply. That lump turned out to be a benign cyst.

So did I immediately rush off to the doctor? No! I was busy moving. I didn't give the lump any negative energy.

A few days later my friend Chris (who had lost a breast to cancer), called me.

"Oh, by the way," I said in passing, "I found a big lump on my breast – quite fascinating really. One day it wasn't there and the next day it was."

"What did the doctor say?"

"I haven't had time to go, I've been too busy."

"Go to the doctor."

"But I'm sure it's just a cyst."

"Go To The Doctor."

"But…"

"GO TO THE DOCTOR!"

"Okay!"

Went to the doctor - had the ultrasound - had the mammogram – had the biopsies – had the cancer!

Driving home from the hospital after hearing the results, I suddenly started to laugh! I had been chatting to God one second and then there I was joyfully belly laughing.

For me, that laugh was the start of a most amazing, spectacular, exciting, gift-filled journey. I had not one moment's fear during the whole experience. Why would I choose fear? I knew I was absolutely safe. Whether I lived or I died, I knew without a moment's doubt that I was 100% safe.

After getting myself home from the hospital, I thought about why I had created the cancer. Did I actually want to continue living or was I ready to move on? And if I wanted to stay in my body for another few years, what steps could I take to help turn the cancer around?

I knew that in part I had created this cancer from my thoughts. My reaction to certain news items and documentaries create an immediate thought response of "I can't stand it – I don't want to live on this planet any more." I had obviously thought this enough times over the years for the universe to say, "Okay! I hear you. Now here's something that will definitely help you achieve that particular goal if that's what you really and truly want. Now, do you want it, or don't you?"

I lay down on my bed and thought: Cancer was definitely an option. However, if I was going to choose to leave this planet, there were much easier ways to do it.

I thought of my friend, John, who had sat down in the shade, rested his head on his wife's shoulder, and within minutes had left on his next exciting spiritual journey with nothing more than a quiet sigh. Wow! He just exhaled and let go. How beautiful is that? And a friend of my mum's who flew off on her next great adventure of life on a wonderful belly laugh. Fabulous!

"Okay, God – let's get this show on the road. What can I do to neutralize this and let go with love, both my thoughts that helped create the cancer, and the cancer itself?"

I had read that a tumor could disappear by visualizing the removal of it; either by digging, hacking, chipping or burning it out, but I soon realized that that sort of visualization wasn't for me.

Instead, I put on the lounge wall, in big bold print, '**Enjoy the Journey**', and visualized my breast as a rolling meadow covered with wonderful wild flowers, some magnificent trees, lots of birds, bees, butterflies and a babbling brook, while underneath many earth worms turned the small dank areas of earth into the same lush loam as the rest of the 'meadow'. Although I only did it once, the vision of my breast as a beautiful meadow was permanently set in my mind's eye.

I chose to have a partial mastectomy. It was a breeze. I healed rapidly with the help of my wonderful Bioptron healing light.

Staying positive wasn't part of the equation – as I said to people at the time, "I am so far beyond 'being positive'. I Just Am."

I didn't say one affirmation – never saw cancer at the 'big C' – never thought of it as a 'battle', a 'fight for life', a 'life threatening' disease or me as 'a survivor' or 'in remission' (I know I'm healed), or told only one or two of my closest friends, swearing them to secrecy ... because if it was spoken out loud I might die. Instead I told everyone I knew about the fabulous journey I was on!

I was not affected by any fears my friends or family had for me. I knew without a shadow of doubt that whether I lived or died from the experience that I was absolutely fine.

I didn't give lip service to a belief, but instead knew it to be true.

When friends said that they would pray for great success over the cancer, I asked them to see the cancer as burning garbage and that the more garbage that was disposed of, the higher my vibration would be able to rise as all the cancer was, was a dying to the old - old patterns, old thoughts, old fears.

So the gifts that cancer gave me?

1. It was clearly a catalyst to show me just how far I had come in my belief in God, trust, life, death and moving on with grace. It is one thing to believe - it's another thing to 'know'. And I can now say, without hesitation, that I know. All I felt through the whole incident was peace and joy.

2. I felt it imperative that I didn't hide behind any masks - I wanted 'Me' to be seen - no drama - no victim - just the I Am that I am.

3. I felt empowered and in complete balance - imagine that now? Fascinating!

4. The only times that I felt tears behind my eyes was when I saw the love and sorrow shining from the eyes of my friends, because for the first time in this lifetime I was able to truly acknowledge and recognize how much I am loved.

5. I learnt that my belief in God, life, death and all that is, is solid, true and powerful within me.

In fact, the cancer came with a multitude of gifts for me to find, the most important being in humble gratitude to God for my amazing life.

Gaia Sharne Singer is author of *"Genitals, Love and Other Bits and Pieces, Things Our Mothers Never Taught Us and Our Fathers Never Knew"*, (foreword by Neale Donald Walsch included in 2nd Edition), and of *"Better Than a Bandage, Simple Solutions to Daily Health Dilemmas."* Receive a FREE e-book, *"Pearls of Wisdom from Genitals, Love and Other Bits and Pieces"* as a thank you for visiting her site at www.SingingEarth.com. You can e-mail Gaia at Gaia@SingingEarth.com.

The Sacrificial Lamb

Jocelyn Oades

The morning stillness rushed to greet me as I awoke from a long forgotten memory of a past time. This quiet moment before dawn, when the hush of the land feels as if the earth has taken a deep breath in anticipation of the day before her, now spills her sigh as the beginning of the day calls the birds to encourage the rising of the sun.

The morning light was captivating as we held each other close. We were lost in the pure sensation of love. It was time to leave the past behind that had lost its luster to explore the unlimited possibilities that lay ahead.

Peaceful yet fully connected to the pulse of the earth, we packed our belongings and headed south, the hum of the car transporting our thoughts and our dreams on our Journey.

The winding roads following the coast were magnificent thick forest with sunlight dancing through the trees. A sign led to a track 'Cathedral Caves - One Hour Walk.' Our two-year-old son Anton was excited anticipating a swim. Twisting along the pathway through the damp forest, with smells of nature untouched, the sounds of birds and running water, was magical. What a memory would be imprinted on my mind, with such beauty heightening the senses. Leaping onto the cool sand in the shade of the giant trees, the three of us ran toward the water holding hands, delighting in the clarity of the azure blue sea. There was not a single footprint on the sand that did not have our imprint on it and we were blessed. We were young and intoxicated with life.

We left the beach to explore the gigantic caves, their name 'Cathedral' bringing a visual symphony to mind. The water weaving patterns on the waves crept toward the back of the caves. We meandered through each individual cave, not realizing the lurking danger hidden behind each step as the gentle waves silently obliterated our footprints. The magnificent sounds of the wind playing against the high walls of the caves brought the eerie howling of a church organ to life. Still we continued, not realizing that each cave behind was now awash, as the tide was fast filling the empty caverns. Anton was searching for rock crabs when we realized our pathway back was already submerged. That moment of surprise and shock that we were trapped and not in control of our lives anymore made my head spin. Mother Nature had a test for us and the way we handled this test would be the outcome that we would have to live with. How minor all the details of the past felt now and how precious my magnificent husband and adorable son were to me. The power of our love was too strong to allow us to give up. Instead we changed our thoughts and focused on survival with a purpose. In the great course of our destiny, we can either choose to be the victim or the victorious.

We locked eyes, held hands and ran treading water slowing with the force of the waves around us. Bernie hoisted Anton onto his shoulders, as the water swirled knee deep, waist deep, then chest deep.

The minutes felt like hours turning into days. I saw flashbacks of when we were children picking pipis, small shellfish on the shore, and the tide came in on the estuary and we were stranded. Daddy swam across to safety with one of us at a time. The cold numbed our bodies and our father reassured us to be brave, as back he went for the next child. There were four of us altogether. With his brute strength and sheer force of will, we all made it. We huddled together shaking, as he bought our brother across the expanse of raging water to join us.

The slap of the salt water around Anton's body jolted me back to reality, and through visualizing that past encounter, I was more determined to survive. Bernie was struggling against the power of the current and fighting to keep our son above water, while I was thrust against the rocks surging up to meet me.

We emerged from the ordeal battered and choking to find the sun shining. Strange how it all seemed so devoid of color before, as the towering cliffs threw dark shadows on the clutches of the sea. We held each other motionless lost in the thought of 'what if.' Maybe the sea laid claim to those who were held captive, and the appreciation of life was the gift of surviving.

The expansive beach lay empty. Only the sigh of the warm breeze kept us company. Anton fell asleep and we made love again on the sand holding ourselves accountable to nothing, as the freedom and expression of our love locked us together in exhaustion and exhilaration that we were alive.

The afternoon breeze stirred and we headed back through the forest. A strange feeling was following, surrounding us. I could hear Maori voices chanting, a language from my ancestors. It was then the pure white lamb appeared. We heard no sound, yet the moment we saw it, we could hear its loud panicked bleating. Leading us forward, always staying ahead, it kept stopping and looking back waiting for us to catch up. This unusual series of events continued with the voices speaking in the familiar Maori tongue. Only I could hear the voices, but Bernie and Anton were mesmerized by the presence of the pure white lamb. Showing not a trace of dirt, its tail intact, swishing gently back and forth with the incessant bleating, urging us to hurry.

The trek back seemed to last forever, this eerie procession threading through the forest. Suddenly the lamb disappeared into the undergrowth. The voices ceased; there were no sign anywhere of sheep or paddocks, only a deserted roadway and the entrance and sign to 'Cathedral Caves - One Hour Walk', yet it was a journey of a lifetime.

We learned that day that all experiences of the past and the future are connected, held together in our subconscious cellular memory. Each incident is a lesson we must understand for us to learn and grow from. Empowerment comes when we cease to judge experiences as negative. When we see the value and appreciation of each moment, then we truly decide to live without fear and blame. We choose to take personal responsibility for our happiness and show our gratitude that each day is precious. In a moment of fear we can use our past experiences to catapult us forward, to build strength and achieve greatness.

The full significance of the sacrificial lamb was not in my awareness in that moment, or the loss I was to experience in the future. This was a gift of precious extended time, for which I have been eternally grateful.

Jocelyn Oades is a personal mentor through life experience. Being a Reiki Master Teacher, her passion is to inspire people to create living a life of endless possibilities. She is in the process of writing a book of her own life experiences to uplift others called *Flight of the Spirit,* of which 'The Sacrificial Lamb' is a chapter.

Visit www.FlightofTheSpirit.co.nz or email her at info@FlightofTheSpirit.co.nz.

SPROUT the Life You Love!

Sarah Prout

I was fortunate enough to grow up in a creative environment where there was never a dull moment. There were always shelves crammed with art books, my mother playing her grand piano and emphatic discussions about money, needs and desired outcomes. We moved many times to houses that had a gallery or studio attached so that my father could sell his paintings and work from home. Looking back, it was a creative wonderland, which gave me a solid foundation for the inspired path I mapped out for myself.

I would say that I have always been an entrepreneur at heart. At age nine I was screen-printing my own little animal designs onto silk scarves and handkerchiefs to sell in my parent's gallery.

When I was fourteen I would draw pages and pages of brightly colored floral patterns. I would start with a bold black outline and then use markers to fill in the petals with shades of fuchsia, lilac and lime. People compared my work with the vibrant wallpaper designs of the 1960's.

I decided to send my designs to Hallmark to generate the possibility of becoming a freelance designer. I remember the excitement of putting together the package and sending it off in the mail. I never really questioned whether or not they would reject my submission; I just acted out of faith and teenage enthusiasm that one day I would be successful.

Miraculously, after a month or so of waiting (and waiting) for a response, the Hallmark production department commissioned me to design four concepts for gift-wrap and one design specifically for the Easter season. As you could imagine I was trilled and became an instant superstar when my finished Easter designs were on display at the largest department stores in Australia. I gained local media attention and was known as 'Hallmark's youngest designer Worldwide'.

At nineteen, I met the love of my life, Dave who introduced me to meditation. This marked the beginning of a journey that unfolded a whole new world of wondrous possibilities. I began seeing the world through a refreshed pair of eyes. I began to see evidence of how Universal Laws (such as the Law of Attraction) shaped my day-to-day experiences. It's so exciting to think about communing with the Universe through meditation. In my belief, it is the most simple, natural and effortless state to tap into. Scientific evidence suggests that there are also many health benefits to meditation, such as reducing stress levels and bringing about a greater sense of well-being.

The same year I found meditation, I held my first solo art exhibition entitled: 'Dream of the Chrysalis'. Two thirds of my paintings sold within the first three days. The profits paid for my first spiritual retreat where I found myself surrounded by like-minded/spirited people. It was bliss.

At the second retreat in New Zealand, Dave and I decided to have a spontaneous spiritual wedding with all of our fellow meditaters to witness. Dave and I stood with the ocean roaring behind us, just after dusk. The room had been decorated with exquisite tropical flowers. I could feel the sea breeze gently hitting my back. It was truly beautiful, but upon reflection I remember not caring about the consequences of being so young. I just threw caution to the wind and proclaimed that the Universe will never give me anything that I am not able to handle.

I was 20 when I lost my first baby. I was three months pregnant and filled with enthusiasm for the life I had co-created. The day that the scan revealed that its tiny little heart had stopped beating was one I will never forget.

In 2001, Dave and I had an 'official' civil service wedding in our home. I was four months pregnant with our son, Thomas. When he was born I suffered from mild post-natal depression, paired with the despair of Dave being dismissed from his job the same week we brought the baby home. It was a time that our faith that everything would work out for the best was tested. My parents kindly allowed us to live with them until we got back on our feet. It took three long months.

After we were settled again, the entrepreneur mind within me decided to start my own business from home. When baby Thomas would go down for his nap, I would write my business plan. In fact, I became part of a contest where I was paired with a business mentor and the person with the best plan would win the funds to start up their chosen enterprise. This was when the SPROUT® brand was officially born. I planned to utilize my passion for writing with my flair for design and start my own greeting card company.

At age 22, I was a prizewinner in the SHELL Livewire entrepreneurial awards for writing one of the best business plans in the state of Victoria, Australia. The prize money funded my first print run of cards that sold in florists and giftware stores around Melbourne. The business slowly gained momentum and then had to close when I moved to Sweden in 2004.

After the life-changing event of becoming a mother and living in Scandinavia for a while, I gained more clarity about the direction I wanted my life to take when we returned home to Melbourne. I felt the entrepreneurial desire surge within me on a new level. I dabbled with writing and marketing, reading more and more books about motivation and self-development.

My daughter Olivia was born in 2006, the exact same week that I started my degree in Journalism. I discovered writing as a creative art and began thinking about how I could start a business that I truly loved while balancing being an excellent, present mother at the same time.

One of the more difficult tasks as a creative person is to find a way where you don't have to compromise your art just for the sake of money. I tried to think of a business concept where I could incorporate all of my entrepreneurial adventures in jewellery making, visual merchandising, design, writing, editing and my passion for metaphysics. I decided that this concept had to encapsulate everything that I LOVED in order to be a success.

I started SPROUT® Publishing and created an online magazine. It was the perfect way to link all of the things that I was inspired by and offer a space for others to be creative too.

Nowadays, I love to spend time with my children, and then in my own time I utilize the Internet to study, make money and compile an awe-inspiring publication to uplift others.

My advice is to pace yourself and enjoy the journey. Look back for a few seconds and thread all of the lessons learned together to form an exquisite present moment NOW. This will pave the way for a vibrant and exciting future to unfold.

Sarah Prout is the owner of SPROUT Publishing, editor of *SPROUT Magazine*, writer and proud mother of two darling children. She is currently based in Melbourne, Australia. *SPROUT Magazine* sources the best products, guest writers, creative spirits and ideas to help readers align with feelings of opulence and JOY. Submissions are always welcome and advertising is FREE!

Visit www.SproutPublishing.net and email Sarah at editor@SproutPublishing.net.

Law Of Attraction in Action

Alison Trebilco

"Cold moss, it's all over... Cold moss, it's all over..." I repeated this over and over again as I fire walked for the first time across the bed of glowing, red hot coals.

I was in Colorado attending "Warriors Wisdom", a spiritual seminar by renowned author Stuart Wilde.

I was 29 and my husband had just died. The life I knew was over. I needed answers about life and death, and I needed to find me. Stuart said that if we raise our energy, we can attract anything we desire into our life. We simply concentrate, visualize what we desire and feel it as having happened.

I had done a lot of early morning visualizations, so must have had my energy up. I was staying with friends in Los Angeles and was about to fly to Puerto Rico. The travel guide said that "If you want to see the island outside of the main city San Juan, the public transport is poor, so you need to drive. Also, hardly anyone outside the main city speaks English, so your Spanish will need to be good." I had never driven on the right hand side of the road, and couldn't speak a word of Spanish. Going to the airport I told my friends I'd need a driver and interpreter.

On the plane I met a young man from Sydney named David. Also heading to Puerto Rico on vacation, he suggested we share a cab into town. David said he'd been driving around the USA with a friend and actually had a US drivers license. He said this made for cheaper insurance, and I was welcome to travel with him, to share car costs.

Next morning at breakfast as we made travel plans, David excused himself and disappeared into the crowd. He returned a while later with a striking girl with long red hair whom he had invited to come along with us. Her name was Andrea, she was German, and had spent the last six months in the USA learning fluent Spanish.

I just looked upwards and whispered "Thank You." Law of Attraction in action again.

A year later I was a summer camp nurse in Pennsylvania. I had wanted to learn to rock climb a few years prior, but didn't know where to start.

The first thing I saw at this camp was the climbing wall. Here was my chance to learn rock climbing.

One of the guys on the outdoor team was Nate, a natural born climber. His family had a wonderful cabin two hours from the camp, and he knew all the climbing areas within a days drive, but he did not have a car.

I, however, did have a car, "The Wildebeest", my trusty brown Toyota Corolla Wagon. We'd traveled across the United States together.

On our day off Nate and I went climbing. When Nate climbed he was very graceful, while I bumbled my way up the rock, but I loved every minute of it.

When camp ended, I found myself in Jackson Hole, Wyoming, in front of an Outdoor store. By the time I left town, I was the proud owner of a brand new climbing harness, shoes, belay plate, loads of enthusiasm and absolutely no idea of anyone who climbed back home and headed back to Australia.

A week after I got home, I was driving with my father discussing how to find someone who climbed. Dad said he had heard a guy on the radio just that week talking about rappelling at Mount Buffalo, about an hours drive away. He said I should call him to see if he had any information on climbing clubs, so I did and got way more than I bargained for.

A couple weeks later, there I was, at Mount Buffalo 'learning the ropes.' Dave said he preferred to train his own people to avoid bad habits learned elsewhere. It wasn't long before I learned to set up the cliffs and run the rappelling sessions on my own. The early starts on cold winter mornings were more than compensated for by the awesome views from my 'office' atop the cliffs at Mount Buffalo, overlooking the Buckland valley, and in the distance seeing Mount Hotham and Mount Feathertop.

During an herbal medicine lecture two years later, I saw a movie about an ethno botanist studying the medicinal properties of plants in the Amazon jungle. I was so inspired, I knew I just had to live and work in the jungles of South America. That probably explains why I'd seen Sean Connery's "*Medicine Man*" over and over. Never mind that I hadn't finished my naturopathy degree, and I wasn't a botanist, an herbalist, or any other type of "ist." There had to be a way to get there. I just didn't know how.

A breakthrough came the next year when I moved to Alice Springs in central Australia. Joseph, a young man also living in the nurse's home, told me he'd been to Guyana, South America, with a group called 'Youth Challenge International.' They run programs for young people to do community development work, and he was sure I'd love it.

I found myself on the phone to Canada at a ridiculously early hour for an interview. While they had lots of experienced Outdoor leaders, they needed a Medical Coordinator. My immediate reaction was 'Oh God, they want me to pretend to be a doctor in a Third World country, with no facilities and no medical experience.' It was really more of a health consultancy role, not so daunting. Besides, they were offering me a chance to live and work in South America - the chance of a lifetime.

Home became a house is Georgetown, Guyana, shared with seven other eclectic people, hailing from Australia, Canada, USA, and Guyana.

In early February, the Youth Challenge participants arrived. They were divided into in 5 groups to be sent to remote parts of the country. I gave a talk on living in a tropical environment, hygiene, the multiple causes of diarrhea, malaria, chiggers, jiggers, bitey stingy things, dehydration and a multitude of other tropical ills – like I was an expert! My first patient was myself. Having written home about the multiple mosquito bites I'd sustained, it turned out I had a good dose of bed bugs.

I visited remote villages, lush rainforests, amazing flat open plains, and boated down tropical waterways. Later that year as a group leader, I lived in an Amerindian village for 10 weeks. After nine months in Guyana, I had fulfilled my dream to "live and work in South America."

It seems to me that how the Law of Attraction works is simple. You have a dream, you believe in your dream no matter what, and let the Universe sort it out for you. Each of these times, I could never have planned things the way they turned out. The only thing that is asked of you is, that when the Universe presents you with an amazing opportunity, believe it and grab it with both hands.

Alison Trebilco lives in Melbourne, Australia, and is a Life Coach, Health Educator, Registered Nurse and Adventurer.

She runs www.AbsolutelyAmazingLife.com whose aim is to inspire people to take on challenges, achieve their dreams and live a life they love. You too deserve an "Absolutely Amazing Life".

Visit www.AbsolutelyAmazingLife.com or email her at Alison@absolutelyamazinglife.com.

How Would You Spend Your Last Day on Earth?

Melissa Scott

If today really was your last day on earth, I'd bet my every dollar that all your past excuses, blocks and sabotage would disappear in an instant! What would immediately occur is a massive motivation to do what you truly love with the time you have left.

Excuses are my most favorite topic to talk about. Before becoming a Life Coach, my life used to be filled with one excuse after the other. I was the "Excuse queen!" I worked in a job that I hated, I was exhausted from doing too much, I was a people pleaser and I had no energy to devote time to what I loved. I was broke all the time, unhappy and a perfectionist who procrastinated like I was competing for gold at the Procrastination Olympics.

Today, I live the life of my dreams and I have really given up my excuses. I am married to my soul mate, and recently joined the "Mummy Club," having given birth to my glorious son, Cooper. I have also created an abundant business, empowering people all around the world to live their dream life plus I get to do what I love all day long.

The life I live today is full of fun, pampering, abundance and no excuses. Excuses really are the number one reason why we don't achieve our goals. It could be said that anything that stands in the way of you and your goal is an excuse. It might be a darn good excuse, but it is still an excuse.

When you use a lot of excuses, you end up believing them to be true and cut off the infinite supply of possibilities available to you. What I have seen so many times in my coaching practice is that people, if given the opportunity, will play it small in their life. What

I mean by this is that they don't live up to their desires and dreams. Perhaps they don't take the action they need to take, don't pursue the opportunities that surround them, or maybe they don't allow themselves to shine personally and commercially.

The great invention of life coaching is very powerful because it does not tolerate excuses. It calls people forth on a regular basis to be accountable, to follow through and do what they say they are going to do.

Think about some excuses you may have been tolerating in your life. Consider your health, wealth, relationships and career - what excuses are hanging about? And what would happen if you decided to let them go today?

Keep in mind that there are two basic positions in life that we can take. We can be the "cause and creator" of our whole reality or we can be at the "effect." Imagine it like an equation and when you are on the "effect" side of that equation, you are full of excuses, reasons and explanations (all very compelling) for why you don't have what you want. When you are on the "cause" side of the equation, you are 100% responsible for the results in your reality (even the results you don't so much like). This ownership enables you the opportunity to transform your mind and body until you produce the results that you want.

I often ask clients to take out a clean piece of paper, a colored marker and write down this sentence, "I can't do anything about my…" and then ask them to proceed to fill the page and sure enough, all their excuses start piling up. My role is to help them start believing that they can change anything and put all their energy into creating new options and ways to create their success.

For the majority of people, the excuse mentality is so well cemented, it takes a brave heart to be willing to start questioning them as you have been extremely comfortable living with them. You have to remember there are always alternatives, and usually a best-case scenario just around the corner when you really put your foot down and rid yourself of your excuses. If you find yourself saying, "I can't afford it," or "I don't know how to do it," or "I don't have the time," etc. - STOP! At the very least, instead of using your excuse, try saying this instead: "I am choosing not to." What this does is put you back on the "cause" side of the equation.

The unconscious creation of excuses is very compelling and I really have heard every possible excuse there is! Most of you may be aware of your conscious excuses however, I guarantee that unconsciously you have some lurking excuses that even you believe are true.

Often times in life, the unconscious mind can feel backed into a corner with no conscious way of getting out of a particular situation, and so it begins manifesting illness or accidents as a way out. In giving up your excuses, you get the opportunity to go to the deepest level of creation and understand we create and attract everything in our life, including those illnesses and accidents. You might not consciously choose them to happen, and yet they are an unconscious creation and serve as a really good excuse or a really big wake-up call that always has a higher purpose involved.

I've always imagined that coming to planet earth is like a game. You are born with a desired mental, emotional, spiritual and energetic blueprint of what you want to experience in this lifetime. Based on that, you had to set up certain circumstances that would ensure you learned exactly what you chose to learn. This has always made me feel better about my own personal traumas and those of people around me.

Reassuringly, as a life coach, I have been able to see the exact truth of my previous words. I have seen that even the worst experience that happens to us is part of a higher plan. And while in the moment of the negative event we might despair, when viewed in proportion, our whole life is a jigsaw of higher meaning that can be seen... if you look for it.

When you understand that you are the creator of all your events, you will realize there are no excuses, and that everything is a choice.

This mode of thinking helps you to be 'real' in your life, to know yourself and start living a more authentic life of CHOICE rather than excuse.

Get yourself back on the "cause" side of the equation. Even if you don't have the money, time, or know-how, simply CHOOSE what you really want, give up your excuses, and start moving towards your dreams. You will be amazed at how rapidly you attract the very thing, person, scenario you desire. Decide to find reasons for your dream life, invest time and effort in your dreams and live as if every day were your last day.

Melissa Scott is an international speaker, Life Coach and author of *Billionaire Buddha-Manifesting Your Heart's Desires,* in which she shares the step by step process designed to ***empower***, ***inspire***, and ***enlighten*** you back to a place of authentic empowerment. Melissa is renowned for igniting your heart's desires and teaching you how to accelerate success in life and business.

Visit www.EquionxLifeCoaching.com for more information or contact Melissa via email at equinox8@bigpond.com.

Do it For Yourself

Jenni Dean

The Beginning

When I was thinking about how to start off this chapter, I focused on the topic of "the body" and "fitness" and how I managed to combine these two aspects into a great life. Next I asked myself, "How can I help other normal people like me achieve the same goal that I achieved – losing weight and looking good?" You're about to read the answer.

Once I really started to think about it, it wasn't about "the body" and "fitness", it was really about empowerment and my mind, plus how using fitness has helped me get to where I am today.

We spend most of our time doing things for other people – family and work – generally putting ourselves last. What I really learned is that to give your best to others, you need to put yourself first. If you are not "right" in your world, how can you give your best to others?

The past 12 months have been quite a learning experience for me. I have gone through a break up with my boyfriend, relying on food as a substitute, nowhere to live and feeling alone, with no vision of the future. On the opposite end I've lost 33 pounds, look and feel fantastic, and am excited about where I am today, with a clear vision of what I expect in the future.

Why am I writing about my experience? It is because now, 12 months later, I see what I have gone through as the most positive turnaround of my life.

When did I realize all this? It wasn't until I mentioned to a girlfriend, "When is it going to be my turn? Why can't things ever go my way?" She replied, "Now I understand what the chapter in the book means." Of course I then asked her, "What book are you talking about?"

The book was *Wildly Wealthy*. I bought it and read it straight through and then realized I was spending my energy on trying to fix things that didn't need to be fixed. The Universe was telling me to "move on" and change my direction. I must mention that this was around the 10 month period within the 12 months I'm talking about. It took me a while to "get it!"

Once I realized this, things started "going my way", and I got really excited about the future. I also realized that I don't need to know "how" to get there - I just need know that I **want** to get there.

Everything will work itself out.

Motivation

To help me get through the year, I did rely on eating. What I did do that was different (and I believe some of you readers may be in the same situation), is I joined a gym and used the fitness aspect to exert all the nervous energy from the turmoil I was experiencing.

This was my motivation, and what I didn't understand was that my body started to change without my noticing it... and for the better. Everyone started to comment on how great I looked, particularly as I was eating more than I ever had before. So this gave me more motivation to be even more successful in building the "perfect body."

I started to learn how to eat correctly, train properly, and got a Personal Trainer who helped me greatly on this goal. At the time I felt that even though everything else was going wrong in my life, my fitness and eating goals were going great!

Once someone asked my trainer, "What is she training for?", and he replied, "Herself." It was at this point I started to understand that you don't have to train for anything or anyone except for yourself.

I have learned a lot from my fitness training, such as making a good habit out of planning correctly for most things, but mainly that you can achieve anything you if you put your mind into it. Only you can hold yourself back, no one else can. If you don't want to do it, you will continue to find excuses on why you can't do it.

To be honest, what made me really excited is that I found a way to eat lots of food without gaining additional weight, while still maintaining my ideal size. I have finally found a way to be a size 10 and not have to diet! I eat so much healthy food on a daily basis, that I am never full, but never hungry either.

As part of this transformation, I have either removed all negative influences around me (which includes people), or if I can't remove them, I have learned how to cope with them and not let them influence my mindset.

This was a very big move for me, as during this transition there were times where the number of positive people around me could be counted on one hand. Today, as a result of going through this exercise, I have many upbeat people in my life, and couldn't ask for a better group of friends.

I have to admit I didn't do this transformation on my own. I had a motivator, my personal trainer, and have learnt a lot from those positive influences around me, most of which are much younger than me.

He has been a major influence in my life over the past 12 months in helping me make my mind stronger in setting and achieving my goals. His calming presence, whether it is from supporting me in my continuing fitness goals, or in my work or personal life, is invaluable.

He himself has been through so much and has a really strong mind, and I think I didn't really understand that until recently, how the mind is such an important tool in what we all do – whether we succeed or fail.

The Right Direction

I am very much a goal setter now, where before I just "talked it" and never 'walked it." I think I was either lazy or didn't have the courage

– not quite sure on the answer to this one – yet either way I am now on the right path.

Having said this, I have gone backwards on a number of occasions over the past 12 months, but I think what makes it all worthwhile is that I have learned why I fell back into my old patterns, and yet was able to pick myself up and continue to move forward.

I have also learned how to really set goals, such as not saying, "I want to lose 20 pounds within 3 weeks." You need to set realistic goals such as "I want to lose 5 pounds in 3 weeks" instead. I have also learned that it doesn't matter if you gain an extra 2 pounds over holidays such as Christmas (one of the steps backwards), because once you're back on track again, that extra weight will come off. Be and think positive!

I have now stepped outside my comfort zone, which was not easy by the way, to look for employment in an organization that is more suitable to me. Instead of viewing this change with feelings of panic, I now look at this move as exciting.

I feel great that I have come to realize that everything is about "me" and maintaining a positive and upbeat mentality. My desire to help others, which I really love doing, is only achievable if I make sure that I am great first!

Jenni Dean thoroughly enjoys motivating people to set and achieve their goals, whether they are focused on losing weight, becoming physically fit, or simply living their best life possible. For further information on how Jenni's personal experience in empowerment and motivation changed her life, email her at JenniDean@optusnet.com.au.

From Boredom to Bravo!

Evelyn Tian

I've always wanted to aspire for excellence, yet year in, year out, I did the same boring thing, commuting to and from the office. I could predict exactly what I would be doing as soon as I opened the door to my office – Monday to Friday, week after week, then soon, it's pay day. 'Pay day' simply meant I got paid only to be paying bills! Life was non-challenging, boring, predictable, unexcitable, and meaningless - without real purpose. Ever had that feeling? My life felt as if I were living it in slow motion.

Then, one fine morning I told myself - that's it! I want more than just going to work, trading time for money, and getting paid to pay bills! I want to attach meaning and purpose to my life; to be uplifted and energized; to add excitement to my days. Yet most of all, the thought of being able to reach out and share knowledge and skills with like-minded people who want success and achievements, motivated me. Enough was enough!

Ironically, as I walked towards my office that morning, my CEO came forward, greeted and asked if he could see me in his office. The time for confrontation had arrived. I was ready for this challenge and walked across into his office.

"You're the first to know" he said. "I've decided to retire"! He stopped there, looking at my reaction. "Wow!" I thought to myself, "Wish I could too!" After a couple of seconds, "Is this good news?" I asked him. He simply answered 'Yes, I've discussed with the family and they think it's the best thing for me! It will happen a couple of months from now." Obviously, when a Chief Executive leaves, there's a good transition period with clients and the like. Hence, I thought to myself "Great! And what about me?"

I then headed back to my office, and for a moment, yes, only for a moment, wondered and asked myself, "Now what? If I leave, who will take care of all the bills?" Then, as God would have allowed, with a deep sigh of relief, I said, "So what? Just make a decision and keep moving on. Now's your chance too!"

Something came to my mind immediately. I would now have time to volunteer at the Sydney 2000 Olympic and Paralympic Games, which at one time I thought work would be in the way and taking time off for volunteer services was such a "luxury." What an amazing twist of fate!

Back in my office, suddenly my body began to vibrate. Like a sunburst of light, I realized," This is my breakthrough! I have to think big to become big, to act and reach a big goal! I want meaning and purpose, success and achievements. That's the path I want to pursue", and pursue it I did.

After he physically left the office, there were still remaining things that needed follow through. I stayed on with the company for another 10 months before making the BIG move out into the world of opportunities.

With 18 years in management consulting and a background in finance, and three different roles, my coaching business came to fruition. Starting with friends and their children, high school students and those transitioning a career move, I had results. My hidden talents and skills surfaced.

After the Sydney 2000 Paralympic Games, I visited Zimbabwe, Africa. What was supposed to be a 4 week vacation, turned into 6 months. Together with a missionary, we expanded a church school to include children with disabilities, setting up school timetables, putting English language syllabus together, setup a library and much more. I had 200 children's books sent to Africa from Singapore and Sydney. In Tanzania, I presented a paper on The Importance of Sports for Women with Disabilities to a Sports Committee. I visited the School for the Blind in Madagascar, hospitals, and charitable organizations in other parts of Africa.

On returning to Sydney, with the help of a group of professionals, The International Institute of SPORT was conceived. "HANDS for Africa" - **H**elping **A**frica's **N**eedy and **D**isabled **S**urvived – raised funds to provide wheelchairs for disabled African children.

I also continued with performance and personal coaching. I set goals and aimed at furthering higher learning towards achieving bigger goals.

The Path to Success

Successful people have a sound and systematic plan to achieve their dreams and goals. Everything, from changing attitude, environment, actions, thought patterns and language - I reflect on my ultimate desire of aspiring for excellence. Careful planning is important to reap long term success and a stabilized position.

The Game Plan

Envisioning myself five years from now, I have a very vivid picture of who I want to be and how I want things to be at that time. As I start my path to success by creating a plan of action and approach, there are five aspects I focus on, namely: personal, family, professional, financial and social. Successful planning incorporates simplicity, flexibility and objectivity.

Being successful comes from within, starting with your thinking. Competence, determination, focus, commitment, and discipline are some characteristics to incorporate. Focus on strengths and improve on weaknesses. Be prepared for random challenges and unforeseen trials. Having strong core values to withstand challenges that come with each objective is essential. Gratitude - having a grateful heart and be thankful.

Going forward, I make sure that what I do is part of my ultimate professional goal. I look for ways on how to excel and further develop myself by improving communications, being more proactive, enhancing skills with continued education and training, and give my time, skills, knowledge as a volunteer on special projects. I network to build contacts with persons who can help, and in return, I then become an asset to empower others to move forward – not forgetting I was once there too.

Prioritize all your needs and wants. Learn how to invest, save, enjoy the income and be able to give. To be in a position to give financially towards great causes is most rewarding.

Always consider your family, friends and business partners in the social environment. Values in family, relationships, and friends are very important in maintaining a solid network. Remember that we have obligations for these individuals which require time and money.

Properties of Goals - How They Can Also Empower You

Goals must be achievable and specific with a realistic time frame and be prioritized. Take massive action through carefully planned steps, incorporating your core values.

Be realistic not to overextend or consider options that seem vague and pointless. Goals are achievable with excellent performance and finesse. Keep in mind that things done hastily or without effort render less than average results, which might prove detrimental to yourself and others.

Actions will not amount to anything if there is no plan to support goals. Even if it did amount to something, it is just as fragile as a house built of glass, instead of one on a solid foundation.

From boredom to bravo! With what seemed like a long road to success, I arrived at my open window! I can safely say I've walked the journey and as a top performance coach, personal development trainer, public speaker and speaker trainer, I am able to reach out and help empower people to achieve their dreams as well! Today I enjoy the fruits of the decision and massive action I took to boldly move forward.

Evelyn Tian is a published author, personal development coach and public speaker. Her Vision is to bring out the best in YOU and her Mission is to empower YOU to achieve personal success. She has developed exquisite personal development and speaker training programs. YOU too can aspire to excellence and discover your true potential and self-worth.

For her free e-book, visit www.ETquisitePerformance.com or email her at Evelyn@ETquisitePerformance.com about her exquisite training programs.

Dream Your Life, Live Your Dream

Bushra Senadji

I am sitting in my beautiful living room, looking at the extension plans for my home. I am reflecting on my journey and the amazing transformations in my life over the last five years. I am awed and deeply grateful for the magic and miracles that continue to shape my life. It all started with a dream...

Five years ago, I was living in a rental home, working at a job I hated, and going through a final separation from my partner while pregnant with my second child. I now live in my own home, with two beautiful children aged 5 and 8, with plans for a beautiful extension. I also thoroughly enjoy my work, while actively investing in real estate.

How did the change occur?

The transformation started after an abundance workshop I attended a few years ago. At the time, I was about to become a single mum of a newborn baby and a three-year old daughter, and was aching for my own little nest. At the workshop, I dreamt of a nice house in a quiet street, with a park nearby and friendly and helpful neighbors. Shortly after the workshop, friends of mine called me to say that the house next door to them was for sale at a price I could afford. It was also on a quiet street and opposite a park. I felt utterly grateful, and knew then that I was able to create the life of my dreams.

All manifestation processes start with a dream. Dreams are very powerful. When Martin Luther King claimed "I have a Dream..." - a dream for freedom and equality between black and white Americans, his dream was at the time considered impossible. Yet today, America is well on its way to realizing it.

Following are the laws I use to create the life I want. If you follow them, I can promise you that you will achieve your dreams also.

1) Spiritual law

Your dream needs to be in alignment with what your higher self wants for you. Your higher self wants you to grow, evolve, and realize your divinity. If your dream does not support this higher purpose, the manifestation of your dream will leave you feeling unsatisfied, unfulfilled. So when dreaming, allow yourself to connect to the essence of what you want, and ask yourself " Will the realization of this dream support my higher purpose?"

2) Mental law

Know with certainty that your dream will manifest. When Martin Luther King spoke his dream, he said "Know this to be true." As a pastor, he knew the power of the universe was behind him for the dream to manifest.

Does this mean that you can't doubt? Not necessarily! Doubts, however, act as manifestation saboteurs, and can significantly slow down the realization of your dreams.

When you think big, you also need to believe big. If you think of manifesting ten million dollars, and the most you have ever manifested is a thousand, you might have difficulty believing your dream. The advantage of thinking big, however, is that a smaller dream becomes achievable. For example, if you consistently think of manifesting ten million dollars, which you might find hard to believe in your situation, manifesting ten thousand dollars becomes very achievable, and you will be able to manifest that amount. That is still ten times what you have ever been to manifest.

3) Emotional law

Once you know your dream is aligned with your higher purpose, and you strongly know it will manifest, feel as if it had already manifested. Why? Because it has! Perhaps not at a physical level, but certainly at higher vibrational levels. So, what do you feel when your dream is manifested? What do you see? What do you hear? Stay connected with those feelings. The stronger the feeling, the faster the manifestation.

I became pregnant with my second child when natural laws dictated that I shouldn't be pregnant. My desire to have a second child was, however, so intense that I acted as if I was already pregnant. I remember purchasing seasickness pills for pregnant women prior to going sailing. I completely identified with every pregnant woman I saw in the street. I ignored seven negative pregnancy tests, until the eighth one was positive. Without knowing it, I was living the emotional rule of manifesting.

Some people (and I was one of them) passionately hate their job. Unfortunately, the intensity of their feelings only helps to create more of the same, a job they detest.

It is also important to feel utter gratitude for what you have manifested. Gratitude has been referred to as the gateway to manifestation. Gratitude also reinforces the feeling that you have already realized your dream.

4) Physical law

The physical rule requires you to take action. Your dream is definitely manifesting, but it might not be delivered to your doorstep. You might be prompted to go and get it, and you will need to be watchful and respond when prompted. The prompt signs are in the form of ideas or feelings that are generally unusual for you. For example, if your dream relates to creating your soul mate, you might have the idea of joining a particular club that you never thought about. Or someone will give you a pamphlet about a particular event that you suddenly feel very strongly about. Always follow through.

There is another, more subtle type of action that you need to take which I call introspective action. It is not often talked about, but it is, in my opinion, a crucial one. As you dream your future, and feel yourself manifesting your dream, it is very important that you watch your body responses. Is there a contraction that shouldn't be there?

A feeling of discomfort, anything that doesn't feel quite right? These feelings tell you that you are not quite ready to manifest what you are asking for.

For example, recently I was going through the process of manifesting one of my dreams when I felt slightly uneasy. I realized that my pride was creating a resistance to receiving it, and I prayed for the ability and humility to receive. A few days later on a Saturday, I was buying bread at a bakery and decided to pay by credit card as I had run out of cash. It turned out that my card was cancelled by mistake on Friday, and I was going to be penniless until Monday. The baker gifted me a loaf of bread with a kind, compassionate smile. I was so overwhelmed by the symbolic gesture that I burst out crying, and realized this was the answer to my prayer. I was put in a humble position where I had no choice but to receive from others, and I was able to replace pride with gratitude.

This is the process and power of manifestation. So allow yourself to dream, be open to receiving, and happy manifesting.

Bushra Senadji is an internationally published author, university lecturer, Journey accredited therapist and NLP practitioner. She is the director of Essentials Proprietary Ltd, a company dedicated to teaching, healing and promoting care and well being worldwide. Her website, www.ShiningEssence.com, contains a wealth of information, teachings, and free giveaways that will help you connect to your core, and achieve your full potential. You can also contact her and email any questions you have to info@ShiningEssence.com.

Take the Plunge

Anita Marshall

I often get asked if there is any such thing as good debt and my answer is "absolutely!" Debt is scary for most people and rightly so. If you are borrowing to service your lifestyle, then that is what I consider to be "bad debt", and it doesn't take long before you are facing the harsh reality that this can't continue. Your debts are increasing, but your assets are not, and you are getting more and more stressed as time goes on. If you are borrowing for wealth creation and to build yourself an asset portfolio, then that's what I call "good debt."

How do I know this? A few years ago I was not earning enough to pay my existing home loan and other debts. I was borrowing to maintain the lifestyle I felt I deserved, and it wasn't an extravagant lifestyle either. I had a small 3 bedroom duplex with a tiny concrete backyard, a reliable car, a small selection of stylish clothes and I spoiled myself and my son Blake with at least two holidays per year. This is probably more than a lot of people had, but I wasn't earning enough to pay for everything. So my debts were gradually increasing - along with my stress levels.

I had always believed in my abilities and knew I was underachieving, so I started looking around for other opportunities. I had only finished Grade 10 at high school and had been working in the financial field for approximately 16 years. I enrolled in an Advanced Diploma of Business Management, and after I graduated it was cemented in my mind that I wanted to run my own business.

I opened my own mortgage brokerage business – "Advanced Finance Solutions", and operated from my office in my 3rd bedroom. I had enough money from my long service leave to last me three months. If I didn't start receiving commissions by then it would be back to the drawing board. Failing wasn't an option. My Mom and

Dad have always been an incredible support to me so we pounded the streets with information kits. Business started flowing in as a result of our hard work coupled with my determination and passion to succeed.

I believe that success requires strong self-belief. I believed in myself and my ability to succeed. I couldn't afford to be complacent, so I didn't just sit back and wait for the universe to deliver my dreams (even though I knew it would). I needed to fast-track the delivery. Action **and** belief was the key to my success. Your dreams and goals will become reality a lot faster if you work towards them, so I stepped out of my comfort zone. I coupled my "goals" with "strategies" and created "plans", then took "action" steps on a daily basis. I also shared my knowledge with other people and learned from everyone around me - not just from their successes, but also their mistakes. Everyone has a story, so be an active listener and try to pick up a life lesson from everyone you meet!

I began a crazy learning curve and would be up from 4 am studying the variety of products and ways to structure finance for my clients. This is when I became finance and property savvy, and realized that I was in a position to be able to purchase real estate myself without it draining my existing resources. I have always believed that property is an excellent vehicle for wealth creation. The finance side of property can be rather confusing. and for most people the idea of debt scares the hell out of them! The wrong structure or the wrong property can have your money flowing down the drain before you know it. Investment property finance is all about "the correct structure", so that you are not impacting your wallet on a weekly basis while you are waiting for the property to appreciate in value. There is no use trying to make money out of real estate if it's going to mean that you have to compromise your lifestyle or go broke as a result.

There are all sorts of asset creation strategies, but my personal preference is property. I like the idea that I can "see" my property, and that real estate has a proven history for wealth creation. Some of the wealthiest people I know have made the majority of their money through property. The other advantage with property is that you don't usually need a lot of money to get started. In Australia, you can take a mortgage out on a property for a high percentage of the cost of the property, which means that you need little (if any) of your own money to finance the purchase (depending on your circumstances of course). There can also be the advantage of having a tenant who is helping to pay off your property while it is appreciating in value, along with the tax benefits associated with negative gearing.

I now specialize in investment property finance, and teach other people how to structure their finances so that they are in a position to be able to buy property for wealth creation. For multiple property purchases it is important that you work out the structure of your finances from the outset. There is nothing worse than realizing after you have already bought a few properties that you should have structured things differently from the start.

When choosing a property, it is important to do your research and buy in "growth" areas. You can speed up the time it takes for real estate to increase in value by buying in the right area. Finding out which areas the local or state governments have plans for spending on infrastructure and development can be a good place to start.

I have now upgraded my car and have several investment properties. It's not just about the assets or money though – it's "peace of mind and happiness." Blake and I have a wonderful, fun and happy lifestyle. We now live in a gorgeous 4 bedroom home with grass and a swimming pool in the backyard where we enjoy spending time with friends and family. The best part for me is I can finance this fantastic lifestyle without worrying about how I am going to pay for everything. We still have two annual holidays, one of which is always to the Myall Lakes with my brother Paul and his girlfriend Suzie. We take Paul's ski boat and Blake is now fast becoming a skilled wake boarder. This is Blake's favourite holiday of the year and I just love seeing the enjoyment on his face when he is waking along behind the boat. Swimming has always been my favourite thing to do so every time I dive into my pool or into the water on one of our exotic holidays, it reminds me of the plunge I took towards a better future for myself and Blake.

My message to you is that if you are sitting back thinking that you would like to achieve more in your life, then do something about it. If you are not earning enough to finance your ideal lifestyle then start looking for other options. Join me and take the plunge for you too!

Anita Marshall, Managing Director of Advanced Finance Solutions, lives in Port Stephens, NSW Australia with her son Blake. Anita specializes in investment property finance and is in the midst of writing her first book about financing investment properties for wealth creation. She can be heard at seminars throughout Australia speaking on the subject.

For a free copy of her *"Property Vision Workbook"*, please email anitamarshall@bigpond.com. For more information visit www.AdvancedFinance.com.au.

LIFE CHANGING DREAMS

Rose Smith

In 3 days time I'm off overseas again! I can't wait to have a break from work! We are just so amazingly busy, I can barely keep up. We just had our supposedly quietest month of the year – January - and what happened? I checked and rechecked the figures, and even my accountant checked the figures as I was certain there was an error. Something must've gone wrong - this has never happened before. Guess what? We were 30% up in revenue! I am amazed we are flying!

How did this happen? Let me backtrack a bit, so I can tell you how I own and operate one of the largest and most reputable psychic networks around, www.AbsoluteSoulSecrets.com.

In September 2000, I had a very strange dream, but that's nothing new. I always have strange dreams, but this one was different. Michael, the Archangel, appeared before me and wrote something on my forehead in white light as I slept. I was in total awe of what I had seen - this visit from an angel. Not just a run of the mill, standard garden variety angel, but an Archangel! He was seven feet tall, broad shouldered, with a ruggedly handsome face and the hugest pair of white feathered wings one could ever imagine. He got my attention! So much so that his image is indelibly etched upon my mind even now, nearly eight years later, and I still feel those same goose bumps. His image will be with me all my life.

At first I didn't know what he had written, and then suddenly I was outside my body looking down at my own face. I saw the words "Absolute Soul Secrets" written on my forehead. When I awoke dazed and awestruck, I pondered this. What were Absolute Soul Secrets? What did it mean? I talked about this to many people, and in fact almost drove my husband crazy talking about! What did it mean? I had no idea.

I tried to relate it to our dire financial circumstances at the time. My husband had been doing contract work in Broadcast Engineering. There were contracts in the pipeline which were cancelled and we were waiting for more contracts to materialize. We had been waiting for months, nine in fact, yet there was no work around anywhere. We hunted and did everything we could think of to find work, but it's very difficult in a small country town. I had psychology qualifications and had previously worked as an emotional therapist at my local women's health centre, and had taught counseling and ethics at a university. However these well paid positions are scarce and don't necessarily appear when you're in financial stress. I was thinking about moving to Sydney, a 7 hour drive away, to work as an emotional therapist, then return on weekends to the area, home and husband I loved. Our savings, which we had been living on, were fast dwindling away to nothing.

So given my background and current circumstances, I couldn't relate the words Absolute Soul Secrets to anything! A few months went by and I had another dream. I had been thinking and talking about these words incessantly. All this time, my subconscious was doing its thing, mulling over the incident, digesting the event and opening me up for more. One night a very small, simple little dream occurred. It was just a voice saying "It's a business." I woke up with a start saying "What business?"

A week later, an ad appeared in the employment section of the Sydney paper I had been scanning for counseling work. Obviously in the wrong column, it was an ad for psychic work. "Work on the phone from home" it said. "Well, I'll give it a try" I thought. I had been interested in psychic readings and paranormal phenomena most of my life. I used to read tarot cards for friends, but I didn't think I was good enough to get a job doing psychic work and I had no professional experience. But I was desperate. It was either this or move to Sydney.

I tentatively called the number, with hands shaking, trying to steady my voice as I spoke. Luckily I have quite a good phone voice so I could cover up my nervousness. Within a few minutes the woman wanted me to do a psychic reading for her. I was completely unprepared for her request, but it happened so quickly I didn't have time to get anymore nervous than I already was. I did a reading for her which wasn't bad, but not great either. I picked up a few things about her personal life that I was circumspect about, and she thought it was great and gave me the job on the spot.

It was a terrible job for various reasons. I left after one week and then had great difficulty getting paid, but I had a new found confidence I could do this type of work. I had this ability and I hadn't even realized it. I could make money from my own natural talents. All my life, I had been relying on my intellectual ability instead of my natural god given talent.

Then it hit me like a Mack truck. This was to be my business! This was Absolute Soul Secrets in the making! My own natural psychic ability had been a secret to me all my life! Immediately I realized what I was meant to do. I had to start a business doing psychic readings. I immediately used the remainder of our savings for set up costs and advertising expenses for my new purpose.

To say the least, my husband wasn't keen. We argued and I clearly remember saying "Well, what should we do? Sit around and do nothing? I have to try! I've been given these dreams for a reason!" That stopped him in his tracks as I had been talking about these dreams for months. Despite my fears of starting a business, I was compelled to act.

By December 2000, my business was ready for the general public. The first week I made $200 profit by placing one ad. The following week I used the $200 and booked more ads. I made $500 and every week my business grew. In fact it doubled its turnover every year. I hired other talented psychics as I couldn't keep up with demand.

Today we have 37 people working with us, relying on us for their livelihoods.

And why? Because I listened to a dream. I dissected it, analyzed it, and almost drove everyone mad with it, but in the end I acted on it. I found the business I was supposed to be in - my niche in the world. My place, my dream. You too can find your special place in the world.

Pay attention to your dreams. Write them down, talk about them. Learn the language of your dreams as there are hidden treasures there for you. You can follow your dreams and be successful. It is your God given right to discover your talents and build a new life around them. They are your gift to the world, and this world needs your creativity. It needs your skills. It needs your passion. Do it!

Rose Smith, BA, DRM, ATMS, Licensed Pilot and Psychic Channel has been an emotional therapist and psychic for more than 20 years. On the strength of a dream in 2000, Rose started an international psychic organization. Today this network helps 1000's of people throughout the world. You too can make your dreams a reality!

For a free report on working with your dreams, visit www.AbsoluteSoulSecrets.com/remember_your_dreams_report.

Call Australia 1300 850 196 or New Zealand 0800 934 733.

Changing the World
One Pencil at a Time

Mike Pickles

In the summer of 2000, I willingly departed the comforts of Nova Scotia, Canada in exchange for an eye-opening, life changing opportunity to participate in an educational development project in Guyana, South America, on behalf of the Canadian Teacher's Federation. The assignment was called "*Project Overseas.*"

The name Guyana is an Amerindian word meaning "*Land Of Many Waters.*" It is the only country in South America with English as its official language. Not surprisingly, it is famous for its Kaieteur Falls, measuring five times as high as Niagara Falls. I highly suggest you pay Guyana a visit ... it's a beautiful country.

Our six week assignment was to help improve the teaching methods of Guyanese teachers. Specifically, we were responsible to help them prepare for their up-coming teacher certification examination. Passing this exam meant a pay increase, and since so many lived in poverty, passing was a major priority.

As I sit here and reminisce about my incredible learning experience in Guyana, I find it hard to believe it was eight years ago. I can still vividly recall the day I was eating lunch with the other Canadian teachers, when a convoy of large, military looking trucks pulled into the schoolyard. We all stopped eating and rushed to witness what was happening.

Once parked, the drivers rushed to the back and pulled up the worn, dust-covered tarps. We could not believe our eyes. Hundreds of people exited from the backs of each of those trucks. "Who are these tired, sick looking people?" I asked. Our Supervisor pointed out that they were the Guyanese teachers. They were the teachers who had traveled hundreds, even thousands of miles to be our students.

I was amazed and impressed with the tireless dedication of these teachers towards life-long learning. Many of them made the long journey with their entire families, had not eaten in days, were cramped beyond endurance, and endured the journey through physical illness. They truly understood and appreciated the value of an education. Now **that's** dedication.

Soon all the teachers were unpacked, showered, fed, settled into their quarters and ready to begin classes. The first two weeks were full of lectures, notes, and assignments, which I had planned in advance in the comfort of my own home. I really felt as though I was making a world of a difference in the lives of these less fortunate, less educated Guyanese teachers. Then suddenly all that changed.

One rainy afternoon, I was slowly packing up my teaching supplies when I was distracted by the voice of a woman. As I turned around to identify the soft spoken voice, I saw the face of an older woman. In fact, I was certain she was young in age, but she looked much older. Maybe it was due to life's burdens and hardships, I wondered. She politely approached me, her eyes staring at the floor as if she was ashamed. I stood there silently and waited as she walked towards me. Finally, she stopped in front of me and asked one simple question, a question which would forever change my core beliefs.

"Do you have one spare pencil so that I may break it in half and give it to two of my students?" Not five, not ten, but one pencil is all she asked. Those words brought tears to my eyes. Not having a pencil to offer, and not knowing exactly what to do, I absently searched inside my wallet and gave her a "Hug Someone You Love Today" card. She smiled, looked at the card, gently took it from my hand, hugged me lightly and slowly walked away.

As I watched her leave the classroom, I realized something very important. It struck me how materialistically rich we are in North America, but often spiritually poor. I realized that although we North

Americans may have far more money to spend on our educational system, those so called less fortunate teachers had one very important resource to offer their children ... their love. This and other incidents of kindness and sincerity in Guyana left me convinced that these teachers truly love their students and they truly love to teach. I promised myself that I would take this experience back to my teaching, back to my students. I had to do something. In the words of Helen Keller, "*I am only one, but I am still one. I cannot do everything, but I still can do something. I will not refuse to do the something I can do.*"

There is no doubt in my mind that the Guyanese teachers did learn from us that summer, that we did increase their pedagogical knowledge and improve their teaching skills. Fortunately for me, I learned just as much, if not more from them. I left all my teaching materials there and I proudly returned to Canada with so much more to offer my students ... more love and hope.

I would like to conclude with a story of the Chinese bamboo tree, which I read in a book from my favorite author and speaker, Zig Ziglar. The Chinese plant bamboo; they seed; they water and fertilize it, but the first year nothing happens. The second year they water and fertilize it, and nothing happens. The third and fourth years they water and fertilize it, and still nothing happens. The fifth year they water and fertilize it, and sometime during the fifth year, in a period of approximately six weeks, the Chinese bamboo tree grows roughly ninety feet.

"Did the tree grow ninety feet in six weeks or did it grow ninety feet in five years?" Of course it grew ninety feet in five years with the constant nourishment and the unfaltering devotion of the farmer. Now imagine your students as the bamboo seed and you, the teacher, as their water and fertilizer. In your hands, you hold the seeds of failure or the potential for growth. What a huge responsibility, but what a great privilege as well.

Personally, there is nothing else that I would rather be doing with my precious time than offering hope, self-improvement, motivation and re-energizing both myself and others in life. This is why I decided to start my own educational-motivational business called "*Educate & Motivate Seminars.*"

I hope that reading this chapter was as entertaining and educational for you as it was for me to write. However, this writing was not simply meant to educate or entertain you, but rather to offer you inspiration. Life is meant to be lived. So go out there and challenge yourself. Make mistakes, travel, read, inspire others, and live life to the fullest. Just don't forget to be kind to yourself, your family and friends, and to the environment along the way.

Until our paths cross again, remember what Ralph Waldo Emerson once said, "*What lies behind you and what lies before you are tiny compared to what lies within you.*" The next time you feel like giving up, think about the Chinese bamboo tree or think about those dedicated, persistent Guyanese teachers ... and don't forget to carry a few EXTRA PENCILS!

Mike Pickles (BA, BEd, MEd) has been teaching for 14 years in Canada, twice in South America and once in Africa. He is also the founder and owner of "*Educate & Motivate Seminars*", delivering educational and motivational seminars and workshops. He is currently teaching in Nunavut with his amazing three year old son Sebastian, but is originally from Halifax, Nova Scotia, Canada.

Mike may be contacted at 416-528-3329 or at mike_sabbie@yahoo.ca.

THE SEVEN STEPS TO SELF-TRANSFORMATION: COMING HOME

Kim Le

1) **To Acknowledge** –
Acknowledge where you are physically, emotionally, mentally, and spiritually at this state in your life. What are the negative emotions that cause you to suffer right now?

When I was married, I had three young children (Christine, Daniel, Roger) to care for while I was working full time. It was a challenging task. (Now looking back, I don't know how I did it.) Each morning I would get my children ready to take them to the babysitter before going to work as a bank teller. After work I would rush to the babysitter to pick up the children, and then hurry home so I could cook two to three course meals. After dinner, around 9:00pm, I did the dishes by hand, and then took a quick shower before going to sleep.

Sometimes my son Daniel had asthma attacks, so I would have to take him to the hospital for his treatment, which could take from 3 to 5 hours, and I would often stay overnight at the hospital. Every weekend I visited my brother who was hospitalized in Napa. He had schizophrenia and later developed bone cancer. He died in 1993 at the age of 20. Because I was giving so much, I did not know how to take time out to care for myself. I became angry and resentful of my husband and we grew apart.

Later I learned to love and honor myself, to take time out for myself, and set good, strong and healthy boundaries. I had to let go of my unhealthy relationship with my husband, and we divorced so I could be healed and become whole again.

When you are angry, sad, depressed, not being heard, not being loved and respected by others, ask yourself why. Be patient to process your thoughts and have a pencil and paper to capture them.

When you recognize how you feel and what causes it, you can change it. Otherwise you will experience the same issue again and again. Ask yourself what you can learn from these situations.

2) To Forgive –

Give yourself permission to forgive others who may have done harm and caused you to suffer.

After I recognized my negative emotions and the cause of them, I decided to take full responsibility for my well being. I am no longer being a victim, and have learned to forgive my husband for all the physical and verbal abuse over fifteen years of marriage.

When you learn forgiveness, you cut the energetic cord between you and the others who have caused you to suffer. Their energy no longer affects you. You will be neutral when you have contact with that person.

3) To Let Go –

As you let go of the person or the situation, you are clearing your emotional, mental, and spiritual bodies to make room for learning and growing.

Once I realized that I was giving too much and he was draining my energy, I forgave my ex-husband and I was able to let go of him mentally. If I hadn't, the negative thoughts and energy would have consumed me. When I was married, I didn't know how to say "NO", nor did I know how to ask for what I wanted. I didn't know how to take time out to recharge. That is why I was depressed and angry. Now I have learned to be more receptive, to be true to how I feel.

You can begin to make sure that you are at peace and balanced in body, mind and spirit by taking three deep breaths to ground yourself.

Once I let go of my husband's past deeds, I was able to see and talk to him and remain grounded and centered.

4) **To Accept** –
I accept the perfection and the imperfection within me. I have learned to be patient, kind, and gentle with myself.

I notice that my clients who do not accept themselves are often very hard on themselves and their loved ones. They have set high standards and expectations, so they expect others to do the same. They always have to be right. Most often they set themselves up for disappointment because no one else can be perfect.

When you are a perfectionist, you merely look for the "right and wrong" in any situation and you miss the lesson behind it.

5) **To Love** –
It took me a long time to understand self-love. I loved my family, my children, and friends, but not myself. When I studied at Brennan Healing Science School, one of my teachers asked the class, "How good you are with self-love?" I was shocked; I had never heard that before. I asked her what she meant and she explained, "What is your relationship with yourself? How are you doing with self-love?"

It took me a while to get to know who I am. Everyday I made a conscious choice of chanting the words "I love myself" continuously, until one day I actually felt the love for myself. It was a wonderful experience. Now I love myself unconditionally. I am at peace with my body, mind and spirit; my whole being is at peace.

6) **To Surrender** –
Whenever I try to control another individual or judge him or her, I know that I am not in balance.

I have learned to surrender by letting go of the person, and I try to put myself in the other person's perspective. I analyze their family traits as it helps bring more love and understanding into the situation. I surrender to the outcome. I know that I love to learn and I will continue to love, learn, and grow to the very end of my life journey.

The process of surrendering – emptying your body, mind, and emotions, and letting go of things or people that have been holding you back, will allow the outcome to reveal itself in an organic manner. The wounding and the suffering that you carry is not who you are. You do have the choice to change it.

7) **To Create** –

Once you have committed yourself to the process of Self-Transformation, you will find that it is time to create and reinvent yourself. If there is something that you do not like about yourself, then change it. You must have love and compassion for yourself in order to become whole and complete.

I am grateful for my life and everything that I have. I have three wonderful children and I love what I do. My clients have become my extended family and I love them all.

I would like to thank everyone who has contributed to my success. I am committed to bring love and light to everyone who needs my help.

I wish for you a life journey full of miracles, joy, love, peace and financial abundance.

Kim Le has studied at Brennan Healing Science, World School of Massage, Yuen Energetic Medicine, as well as Energy Medicine with Dr. Sha before opening **Nurturing Spa for Wellness** in San Francisco's Marina District. Kim's Healing Touch Therapy and monthly Crystal Singing Bowl Meditation circles bring delight, prosperity and inspiration to many. She is committed to bringing love and peace to the world.

Please visit her website at www.NurturingSpaForWellness.com or email her at Kim@NurturingSpaForWellness.com.

Zachary's Lessons

Larissa Zimmerman

For those who have recently lost a loved one, may you find hope in the following words. For those who have not yet lived through this experience, please appreciate your living loved ones now. What follows is a snapshot of my life two years after a life changing event. Thankfully this happened for me at the age of 32. I'm so glad I didn't have to wait longer to realize that I hadn't truly taken stock of what was important in my life. I have since learned that the quality of my life is determined by the quality of my questions and so now I ask you:

How is it that we can go through life experiencing the death of a much loved one and yet, continue to enjoy our own life to the extent that we can laugh again and feel absolutely brilliant?

Depending on your experience, you may not believe that you will be able to laugh or feel brilliant ever again. Indeed I had that very belief too. On April 27, 2004, my 26 year old brother gassed himself to the song "Cry Little Sister" from the Lost Boys Soundtrack. While I remember vaguely what happened next, I realize now I went into a state of shock which lasted to some degree for a few months. Even today I sometimes find it hard to control the crying that results from that inexplicable feeling of having your heart ripped from your body. Ironically, it seems to hit when my spirits are highest and I'm suddenly overwhelmed with the thoughts of my loved one: How could he leave this wonderful world and was there anything I could have done? I remember having been in that space myself many years ago, and all I really wanted was to stop the pain. I just wanted to 'get off the bus' for a while, not necessarily stop the journey altogether.

While I don't know exactly what my brother was thinking that day, I do know his parting words were "I love you", written on the whiteboard in the kitchen. I never knew him to wish anyone harm and sometimes I think his passing reflects Darwin's theory of survival of the fittest, meaning he was too sensitive for this world. As I type this four years later, my eyes still water, partly due to sadness for a brilliant musician who struggled to cope and gain acceptance and partly because his passing has taught me to follow my own dreams with such vehement passion, that I now find one of those dreams, being published, coming true.

Of course the deep pain of losing Zachary will be felt for the rest of my life, and in the lives of our family and friends. However, the raw wound slowly, ever so slowly at times, does heal if you allow it. Having developed a positive attitude to life before this event, my healing was helped by asking what positive lessons I could learn from this tragedy, although I could not find any answers to this question initially.

At the time my way of dealing with this wound was to read all I could find, and talk to as many people as I could about "it." I wanted to dissect "it" so I could understand, and I wanted to prod at "it" like I would an aching tooth. You know, how if you keep pressing the gum, eventually the searing pain just becomes a dull ache you can bear. Well, here are the lessons I found from that prodding.

There is at least one positive to every negative. It's nature's way for balance. It's easy to get stuck asking "Why?", but ask yourself "Do you want be stuck forever?" By asking quality questions you can find your way out of the fog with profound insight.

You can't always be in control and the harder you try to be, the longer the healing process will be. Sometimes it's healthy and helps the healing to feel weak. While it may be very hard, you can choose to work through your grief to see the positives. But avoiding some of the hurt, burying it deep down, will not allow you to fully release the pain and feel the happiness that is on the other side of grief.

Embarrassment is one of the hardest feelings to overcome and really only happens when we care what others think. Sometimes not caring is a good thing, as it allows true expression to come forth.

They say what doesn't kill you makes you stronger. This is true, but there can be a terrible time of feeling like a failure and loss of self-confidence before true strength presents itself.

If someone looks up to you, recognize this and let them know that they are also a wonderful person.

There is no right or wrong way to grieve and you cannot compare your grief to someone else's. Everyone is different, as is their relationship with the deceased. Just because someone doesn't outwardly show their grief, this doesn't mean they're not bleeding internally.

Don't wait for someone to ask for help. Cultivate a generous nature and offer assistance before it's too late.

Take photos and videos of those you love. Capture their voice, their laugh and any little thing that is just so them.

Never be in too much of a hurry to talk to those you love and always end on the best possible note. If you don't, it may be the greatest regret of your life.

Hug and love like there's no tomorrow. A strong hug has amazing healing qualities, as does putting your thoughts on paper.

There is always someone with a worse experience than your own.

Never mock someone's dreams. Discuss them and appreciate that the world would be boring if we were all the same.

Some people are unfortunate in going decades without a life changing experience. I'm grateful I've had to question my beliefs to gain clarity. I now have a new perspective of things not going according to plan and have developed coping mechanisms to deal with other critical incidents.

No amount of money can bring back a loved one who has passed. However, it is helpful to have enough money so you can say to the world "Just forget about me for a while, while I spend time with those that are important and heal myself."

If you love, lose and learn, you haven't really lost. Death is a part of life and we will all experience the grief of losing someone. One day that someone will be you. Aim to give all that you can to those you love and have them know that when you are gone, they are to be happy that you have shared a wonderful relationship. We were not put on this planet to be alone.

Be grateful for the smallest joys in life and smile. It's a physiological reaction. You can't help feeling better, even momentarily, and then it's like the snowball effect. Just like the compounding grief where each little negative appears bigger, the positives will eventually grow into laughter and fun.

Sincerely wishing you great happiness.

After years in the Army, **Larissa** chopped the hair, bought the motorbike, got eight part time jobs, developed a simple budgeting process and went into business to help others. Her qualifications and energy have her delivering Health and Wealth courses for all ages, and she is possibly the first Australian to study Financial Services Consumer Education. For a Healthy Mind, Body and Wallet, visit www.FinancialFitness.com.au or call 1300 YES NOW (1300 937 669).

Inspiration: Your Ultimate Calling

Dr. Wayne W. Dyer

I'm going to give you 12 very specific tools to simplifying your life. Begin using them today if you're serious about hearing that ultimate call to inspiration.

1. Unclutter your life. You'll feel a real rush of inspiration when you clear out stuff that's no longer useful to your life. In the words of Socrates, "He is nearest to God who needs the fewest things."

2. Clear your calendar of unwanted and unnecessary activities and obligations. If you're unavailable for Spirit, you're unlikely to know the glow of inspiration. If you're grossly overscheduled, you're going to miss these life-altering gifts.

3. Be sure to keep your free time *free*. Be on the look-out for invitations to functions that may keep you on top of society's pyramid, but inhibit your access to joyful inspiration. Begin declining invitations that don't activate feelings of inspiration.

4. Take time for meditation and yoga. Give yourself at least 20 minutes a day to sit quietly and make conscious contact with God. Begin a regular yoga practice – you'll feel healthier, less stressed, and inspired why what you'll be able to do.

5. Return to the simplicity of nature. There's nothing more awe inspiring than nature itself. The fantasy to return to a less tumultuous life almost always involves living in the splendor of the mountains, the forests, or the tundra; on an island; near the ocean; or beside a lake.

6. Put distance between you and your critics. Choose to align yourself with people who are like-minded in their search for simplified inspiration. Your life is simplified enormously when you don't have to defend yourself to anyone, and when you receive support rather than criticism.

7. Take some time for your health. Consider that the number one health problem in America seems to be obesity. How can you feel inspired and live in simplicity if you're gorging on excessive amounts of food and eliminating the exercise that the body craves? Recall that your body is a scared temple where you reside for this lifetime, so make some time every single day for exercising it.

8. Play, play, play! You'll simplify your life and feel inspired if you learn to play rather than work your way through life. I love to be around kids because they inspire me with their laughter and frivolity. By all means, get back in touch with your real, playful self and take every opportunity to play!

9. Slow down. One of Ghandi's most illuminating observations reminds us that "there is more to life than increasing its speed." By slowing down, you'll simplify and rejoin the perfect pace at which creation works.

10. Do everything you can to eschew debt. Remember that you're attempting to simplify your life here, so you don't need to purchase more of what will complicate and clutter your life. If you can't afford it, let it go until you can.

11. Forget about the cash value. I try not to think about money too frequently because it's been my observation that people who do so tend to think about almost nothing else. So do what your heart tells you will bring you joy, rather than determining whether it will be cost-effective.

12. Remember your spirit. When life tends to get too complex, too fast, too cluttered, too deadline oriented, or too type A for you, stop and remember your own spirit. You're headed for inspiration, a simple, peaceful place where you're in harmony with the perfect timing of all creation. Go there in your mind, and stop frequently to remember what you really want.

Dr. Wayne W. Dyer, Ph.D., is an internationally renowned author and speaker in the field of self-development. He's the author of 30 books, has created many audio programs and videos, and has appeared on thousands of television and radio shows. Dr. Wayne Dyer is affectionately called the "father of motivation" by his fans. Despite his childhood spent in orphanages and foster homes, Dr. Dyer has overcome many obstacles to make his dreams come true. Today he spends much of his time showing others how to do the same. When he's not traveling the globe delivering his uplifting message, Wayne is writing from his home in Maui. For more information, please visit www.DrWayneDyer.com.

WORKING MIRACLES

Enza Lyons

When 5 year old Ella came to see me, she didn't like playing on swings or riding over bumps because it made her dizzy and feel sick to her stomach. Her mother Gina told me that at school Ella was slow to catch on to new concepts, found it hard to sit still and had poor concentration. In fact, her parents deliberated whether she should go on to grade two because she was struggling and was so tired.

Ella had previously been to an occupational therapist who found she had auditory and vestibular processing difficulties which affects balance, vision and learning ability. She was recommended to see me as I can assist people with overcoming learning difficulties, coordination and balance problems.

When I first met Ella, I asked her to read for me, which she did, but very slowly. During that first session I worked with her to integrate the body's primitive reflexes, stimulate the whole brain and balance the body through kinesiology techniques and exercises. Amazingly, by the end of the session when I asked her to read to me again, her flow of words was considerably more fluent and she wasn't feeling queasy any more.

After several sessions, Ella's reading jumped many levels and we were all so excited to see a big change in her balance, concentration and communication as well, in such a short period of time. Since then her parents have seen remarkable improvements in many other areas of her development.

Ella is a shining example that people of all ages can start taking charge of their life and to actively reduce their stress levels. They can be empowered and don't need to feel helpless.

As a registered Kinesiologist, everyday I see inspiring people like Ella, both young and old, who have benefited from the simple yet effective exercises and techniques of kinesiology that I use with my clients.

It's so encouraging to understand how the body works and to see the outcomes of connecting and integrating the brain and body, growing new neural pathways, and reprogramming the stresses and trauma that become locked into our muscles. I've seen people reduce their dizziness, pain and stress levels, significantly improve their learning, alertness, productivity and performance, and overall gain a greater sense of wellbeing.

My first experience with kinesiology was 25 years ago after I gave birth to my daughter Michelle. I had lingering lower back pain for seven months, and going to the chiropractor just gave me temporary relief. Someone suggested I see a kinesiologist, a practice that was very new in those days. I did and I came out of the session feeling free of pain for the first time in months.

I was so excited about this study of body movement that I started to learn as much as I could about it. At that time there was no one in Australia teaching it and I had to wait for experts from the United States to come to Australia. It was Dr. Paul Dennison who finally introduced me to Brain Gym® which is part of Educational Kinesiology. During the course he did a 'balance' (like a tune up) on me as a demonstration. Afterwards I felt fantastic and free in my body. It was just an incredible experience and I was so excited. I wanted to help others reduce their stress levels and help them feel like I did - relaxed and alert.

I began to understand that too often we only use parts of our brain as opposed to a whole functioning unit. Once we integrate all parts of our brain - front and back, left and right, top and bottom - we literally 'switch on' the brain, and immediately we can start reducing our stress, program our thoughts to new positive levels and change the way we learn.

When we experience stress, we only use part of our brain. When we use our whole unit, we look at life more positively, are more creative, courageous, assured and innovative. I've worked with people in all areas of life, especially with people experiencing depression and anxiety. It comes down to how we deal with stresses and traumas. We don't need to get stuck and can learn to follow our dreams.

Another story I remember well is of 12 year old Jack who had been taking medication since he was four years old for ADHD (Attention Deficit Hyperactivity Disorder), which plagued him with inattention, hyperactivity and impulsivity. His mother wanted to take him off the medication, but was afraid of what might happen with his erratic behavior.

When I started working with Jack, I found there was delayed development in his primitive reflexes (reflex actions exhibited by normal infants), and also his postural reflexes. I taught him Brain Gym® exercises to help him take charge of his emotions and become more cooperative.

Incredibly, by our third session, his mother Juanita was able to take him off the medication he had been on for eight years. Since Jack had being doing Brain Gym®, he was able to control his behavior and felt more relaxed and energetic. And more importantly, he was able to handle responsibilities with maturity. It's amazing how once his brain and body began working together, many areas of his life improved including his reading, writing, coordination, breathing, communication and ultimately, his confidence.

The wonders of kinesiology are not only for young children, but for students, parents, business owners, teachers, athletes and anyone who wants to reduce stress, pain levels and fulfill their dreams.

A 'balance' session is like a tune up once a month for the body, like a car, to help keep it functioning. It has helped people transform themselves through periods of great stress, such as Kay Walker who I met when she was going through a divorce.

Kay said the first session helped her to relax and loosen up so she could focus on letting go of the past and looking towards the future. After further sessions she commented, "I found it also helped my comprehension in my studies assisting me to achieve impressive exam results. Also, after the death of my Mom, kinesiology assisted me to cope with the grieving process."

Kay is now doing extremely well and is enjoying prosperity and independence. We now meet regularly once a month for a 'tune up' session.

I've also seen the 'balance' session help people become successful in their endeavors such as Stuart Stuart who had dreams of songwriting and producing when I first met him.

He's said, "Since first visiting Enza, I have had the most amazing run of good fortune, good times and good success. I am now working for myself, doing exactly what I want, making a very healthy income and living with a beautiful girl who makes me happier than ever. Enza has helped me find the energy, motivation and the attitude I need to succeed on a larger scale that I ever thought possible."

I just love seeing people like Stuart and Kay being successful and achieving their goals. We are meant to have abundance, contentment, peace, love and joy in our life. It's often a challenge for many to achieve that.

It just fascinates me that I can use simple kinesiology techniques and miraculously the body balances. And that's what inspires me. I love seeing the positive changes in people. It is fulfilling for me to be working with people to assist them to achieve empowerment, motivation and joy to live life to their fullest.

Enza Lyons, registered Kinesiologist, wife, mother and grandmother lives in Brisbane, Queensland. For 20 years she has coached people worldwide to realize their goals through integrating their body and brain to achieve optimum health, motivation and peak mental and physical performance. She has been featured in Australian newspapers, magazines and television.

Contact her at Enza@SmartMinds.org.au, visit her websites www.DynamicLearningandHealth.com.au, www.SmartMinds.org.au, call at 61 7 3279 2634 or write her at Smart Minds, Curragundi Road, Jindalee, Brisbane, Queensland, Australia.

Transformed from Shy Little Girl to Empowered Woman

Jacki Janetzki

I would like to introduce myself. My name is Jacki, a confident woman who finds it easy to assert my needs, speak up for myself, and openly pursue what I want. I believe in myself and am comfortable and at ease with me. I am blessed with a happy, loving family life - a husband I love dearly and two beautiful daughters that I cherish. I live my life with passion, doing the work I love and loving the work I do. Inspiration and creativity come easily to me and I spend my days absorbed in writing "words with impact" – short, powerful statements of self-belief that I share with the world in the form of empowering gifts to help other people shine. I truly believe that my fulfilling life is a reflection of the self-love that I have come to know within. Life hasn't always been this way. My life today is a long way from where I was 9 years ago.

1999 was a year when I found myself crying a lot. I was working at a job I didn't enjoy and the tears were flowing everywhere - at work, family dinners, even hugging my yoga teacher after class! I was desperately unhappy and didn't know why. In hindsight, my symptoms were probably those that the "experts" of today would label as depression. I didn't seek any advice from a doctor, so I'll never know. One thing I'm certain of is that I felt lost, and I didn't know how I would ever find myself again.

My heart is full of gratitude for the direct and caring way my Yoga teacher spoke to me the day that she looked lovingly into my teary eyes and said: "You need a Light-Heart Healing Session." This simple, seven-word, statement changed and maybe even saved my life. I'm eternally grateful that I allowed myself to be guided by faith and trust at a time when I was lacking direction and in desperate need of help. I listened to my heart that day and scheduled an appointment to participate in a form of therapy that I'd never even heard of. To this day I am extremely happy that I did!

Looking back now, I often tell people that "my dam was full." The floodgates sprang open during my first Light-Heart Healing session (a form of healing similar to Holotropic Breathing and Rebirthing), and it felt like I had cried buckets of tears by the time we were done. Never before had I cried so deeply, and when the experience was over I intuitively knew that this process was transformational and I wanted to do it again. I felt an amazing sense of lightness and liberation as a result of being encouraged and allowed to openly express myself. The freedom I felt after expressing emotion was light years away from anything I had ever experienced in the past. As a baby, I was given a pacifier to stifle my crying and whenever I hurt myself in childhood, my parents directed me to quickly contain my noise and tears.

A number of incidents during my childhood involved verbal abuse from various "authority figures" (teachers/parents/aunts etc.), and this resulted in me becoming a fearful little girl who lacked self-confidence. I always felt trapped by my painful shyness, and because I was unaware that tools for change existed, I continued to carry this uncomfortable, introverted identity with me into adulthood. After living a withdrawn life of suppressed emotion for 30 years, I had now found a simple, effective method that gave me the freedom to let go and express the stored anger and resentment associated with events from my past.

I soon came to understand that the breath is the magic key that unlocks emotion from the subconscious mind. Human beings store remnants of traumatic life experiences in our subconscious minds and then trick ourselves into believing that they're safely locked away in a place where they can no longer hurt us. We never, ever want to be faced with these painful memories again, so we go through life thinking that we've either dealt with or forgotten about our issues.

This is when the "I'm okay" mentality emerges and we commence pretending that "It's all good."

I wonder what would happen if we took the time to really consider the idea that our past experiences have a major affect on the way we live our day to day lives. It's my personal belief that the pain of the past is what drives people to indulge in the disempowering behaviors of overeating, smoking, shouting at their children, hitting their spouses, drinking excessively, taking drugs, committing suicide etc. Once I developed a true understanding of the above concept, I became passionate about freeing myself from the emotional pain of my past, and eagerly participated in Light-Heart Healing Sessions every week for the next 12 months.

Little did I know that there was a tiny "being" in heaven watching my transformation and waiting for the right time to join me on Earth. By August 1999, I had cleaned out some of the "old" to make way for the "new" and I became pregnant with my first child. The more I began to offload my emotional burdens during pregnancy, the more space I created for inspiration to flow to me. I began receiving empowering messages of self-belief and commenced writing them down. After a short time, I felt the urge to share these words of wisdom with the world and from here, the idea of a business which designed beautiful gifts and adorned them with empowering messages was born.

As I confronted and integrated incidents in my life that had been the catalyst for my introversion, I slowly began to feel more comfortable in my own skin. I had begun to grow wings and would soon soar. A popular saying in life is: "Shit Happens", and yet I don't ever remember signing a contact prior to my birth stating that I would be compelled to hold onto the residue of that "shit" for the rest of my life.

Releasing the subconscious programming that no longer served me helped me develop new ways of thinking about myself, and this in turn paved the way for a happier life. I can honestly say that my creativity began after I commenced de-cluttering my subconscious mind. My talents were revealed when I released my emotional baggage. Previously I believed that "I'm too shy; I can't do it; I don't know how; I'm not creative etc." These are all subconscious beliefs and I felt compelled to ask myself how they got programmed into my mind. The only true answer to that question is: "I put them there." Phew! How liberating to come to the realization that if I had stored these disempowering beliefs in my mind, then I was the one in charge of removing them. The time had come for me to focus on new thoughts of personal empowerment.

I am so grateful I discovered the other "Secret" to obtaining everything you want from life: "Release your hurts and reveal your love." Do the inner work to change you, and then you'll see your life change.

Jacki Janetzki is a writer who displays her harmonious and uplifting messages of self-empowerment on beautiful gifts. Inspiration comes easily to Jacki and she loves designing Empowering Gifts to share her words with others and help them shine. Jacki offers free Daily Messages of Empowerment, free Empowering Thought Posters and the opportunity to purchase gifts with meaning for yourself and your loved ones at www.EmpowerMyDay.com. You can contact Jacki via email at Info@EmpowerMyDay.com.

METAPHOR POWER: THE MASTER KEY TO UNLOCKING YOUR SUCCESS

Inanna Lawton

Have you ever felt as though you are held back by something deep within, or unable to reach your full potential as a creative, successful, abundant and happy person? And would you love to **BE FREE and break through limitations and blockages**, and just accelerate your success and fulfillment – easily and effortlessly?

Yes, this is exactly what I've experienced. In fact I've had number of issues to deal with. I didn't believe in myself and I didn't feel worthy of success. I thought I knew what I wanted to create in my personal life and business, but I procrastinated and was often unclear and unfocussed.

I wanted to change my life and create more success and happiness, but struggled to manifest it. I did positive thinking, recited affirmations and waited for the magic to happen – but nothing did. The result was self-sabotage, giving up on my vision and dreams, and returning to where I had always been.

Take a moment and ask yourself if you self-sabotage and if you really deserve success? Most of you may say "Yes, I do", but honestly do you really believe it? Everyone wants success. In fact everyone deserves success, but only a few know how to receive and handle it. **Consciously people want to make a change, but often unconsciously undermine the way they think, believe, behave and produce results**.

Our mind processes on two basic levels - the conscious and the unconscious mind. In simple terms the conscious mind is responsible for our immediate life experiences, conscious thoughts and feelings. This is where you do your logical thinking, analyzing and rationalizing.

The unconscious mind holds the memory of all our experiences and is responsible for behavioral patterns and personality structures.

It is the primary motivator behind thought, beliefs, emotions and actions. Within the unconscious are different levels: one part is responsible for automatic body functions, another for universal knowledge and another comes from spirit relating to matters of the soul and giving us divine guidance and insight.

Both levels go hand in hand when it comes to running your life. Sometimes they don't agree, and that's when you experience inner conflict. Understand that **most power is stored in the 90% of the unconscious**, not in the 10% of the conscious mind you are aware of using.

Consciously you want to change a habit or behavior and then you don't understand why you can't achieve the desired change. Sometimes you achieve the result, but eventually you may experience that you slip back into old behavior.

For instance, if you consciously think that you deserve success, but the unconscious runs a pattern of unworthiness, then conflict occurs and the result is negative. Unless you change these unconscious patterns and structures in the deeper level of the mind, the unconscious will prompt you repeatedly to create your life according to them. You are in conflict with what you may consciously think and you have no control over this.

Knowing that so many people face the same issue, I had a personal and a professional interest as a therapist to find an easy and effective way to change these limitations and bring the conscious and unconscious into alignment.

I've tried and studied many different modalities and their impact on shifting these unconscious blockages which hold us back. The break-through was when I learned how to access the unconscious using metaphors. Finally, this was the key to create profound changes and release self-sabotaging patterns rapidly.

I felt major shifts taking place immediately. I felt stronger and took control of my life. I had more clarity, focus, motivation, confidence and determination to accomplish and manifest my vision and accelerate my success. I was goal orientated and nothing was stopping me anymore! I was on my way to creating the life of my dreams.

I also noticed how quickly clients began to experience alignment between the conscious and unconscious, and how much easier it was for them to create their desired results.

So how do we bring alignment between the conscious and unconscious using metaphors?

Research shows that the **unconscious thinks in pictures and images or metaphors**. We encounter metaphors continuously in our lives such as in dreams, art and religion.

Consciously we use metaphors all the time. They influence our language and our thoughts, e.g. we express love in terms of a journey as in "our marriage isn't going anywhere", or when we feel betrayed, we say, "He stabbed me in the back." What happens is that we hear these phrases and connect to the emotions that the phrase conjures up. **Thus metaphors are not only a matter of words, but also a matter of thought and energy**. They communicate emotions, behavior, and ideas.

Have you ever woken up in the morning and wondered what the dream you had last night meant? Sometimes the dream probably didn't make any sense to you. What you recognize as a dream is the unconscious working out your thoughts and emotional states from what happens in your life. This process happens through metaphors.

The key is to know the metaphorical language of the unconscious. Thousands of metaphors and their meanings have been discovered through dream and speech analysis, and they live collectively, universally within us.

Metaphorical visualization is the powerful tool to access the unconscious. It allows us to use the power and force from deep within to change our lives effortlessly.

Here are just some benefits:

- it allows you to process directly at an unconscious level
- it facilitates new patterns of thought, behavior and feeling
- it bypasses normal resistance and defenses

For example, there is the metaphor "wolf." It represents the energy of motivation and protection; another metaphor is the "Earl", representing that part within us that has already achieved all goals and dreams.

Research also shows us that it is important how these metaphors form themselves in the unconscious, because this will have a direct impact on your life.

If, for instance, the metaphor "wolf" appears as a small or sleepy wolf, then you probably find that you lack motivation or you may only get small spurts of it. Specific images within visualizations allow you to alter these dysfunctional metaphors and restore harmony and alignment. **You will find as the metaphors change to normal healthy proportions, so your results will also change**.

Now it's your turn. Read the next section first, then visualize (daily if you want) and increase your motivation.

"Close your eyes, take a few deep breaths and relax. Then have the image of the wolf appear in your minds eye. Have it come up to you. Check out its size, its head should be up to your waist. If it is too small increase its size, or if its too big decrease its size. Then stroke the wolf, really connect to it, and look into its powerful eyes. Take a few minutes for this and see if you notice any energy shift or sensations in your body."

Let me know what happened!

Metaphorical visualization is the most amazing tool for conquering self-sabotage and limitation. You tap into the power of the unconscious using its language and you change your life. You are a Winner!

Inanna Lawton has been working with people therapeutically in personal development for over 20 years. She has assisted thousands of people worldwide to break through their limitations, make profound changes at an unconscious level and changed their lives forever. Inanna is a published author, international speaker, Hypnotherapist, Reverse Speech Master and has a background in behavioral psychology and counseling.

Email her at Info@InannaLawton.com or visit www.InannaLawton.com/ispbook1 and get your free metaphorical visualization valued at $37.00.

THE INCREDIBLE POWER OF FOCUS

Trish Riedel

"The results are positive. You have Breast Cancer."
If you have not heard this little phrase, then you can only imagine how devastating it was for me. To top it off, it was a fast growing cancer and the lump was already 3 centimeters in size.

Your world as you know it stops. For most people a new world of tests, hospitals and possible treatments begin.

100% of my focus instantly turned to me and surviving.

This was almost 7 years ago and I really learned the value of focus. The goal was easy – staying alive and being healthy, but the focus was the real power.

It was like I turned into a mad woman, researching every tiny piece of information on surviving breast cancer and being healthy. Thank goodness for the web as it was my savior. I started to read about people who were in the last stages of cancer. They had tried all the conventional treatments with no success, but had gone on to live for many years using alternative treatments and ideas.

I think I knew deep inside that survival would come from having a healthy body that was in peak condition, and a strong and powerful mind. We each need to decide what is right for us at the time.

My decision was to have my lump removed and against my surgeon's advice, not have radiation and chemotherapy. Trust me, in the early days I often woke up in a cold sweat in the middle of the night wondering if I'd made the right decision.

The real power of focus then came into play. I wanted to get my body into peak condition to fight this disease. As a result of my research, I became a Vegan - no meat, chicken or fish; no eggs, coffee, diary, alcohol and no sugar. My body went through a complete detox.

I look back now and wonder at what I ate, but I did consume super healthy organic produce and felt sensational.

I was lucky as I had the full support of my husband and son. They also became vegans - at least at home. My son was only 15, and this was a massive commitment for a teenager. My husband and I already exercised most days and we continued this regime.

I had always been fascinated with the power of the mind and turned to these concepts to bring about my internal healing. When you ask the question, the answer comes. I found amazing people with a range of remarkable techniques that bought power and focus to the real healing – the inner healing.

What I find really interesting is that although I had this life threatening disease, I never felt sick. I felt fantastic. I had amazing levels of energy and I seemed to be able to accomplish anything. I was completely focused and never once deviated from my eating plan. I practiced my meditations daily and I worked on my inner healing constantly. I remained on my eating plan for a year.

Around the time of my diagnosis, my husband and I were developing our property portfolio, and that was one of the many things that had gone on hold. Because I felt so strong, four months after being diagnosed, I had bought a cheap property in country NSW, sight unseen, over the phone. Prior to my total focus on changing myself from the inside, I would never have had the courage to do this. It was an exhilarating experience.

Just for the record, today I am currently super healthy and intend to stay that way.

But the years have gone by and although I still had a focus on being healthy, I looked up one day and seemed to have lost some of my power. I know it was because I had lost some of my focus. My life was just drifting along, and although I was earning good money, I had had an ambition for some time to run an international eBusiness and teach people about the power that I had unleashed in myself.

It was probably a bit more like a nagging voice in the back of my head.

It was a disappointing realization to me that I had let my focus slip. I had even gotten to the stage where I blamed an external situation. I knew change could only come from within, and that my main complication was that I knew nothing about websites and eBusinesses.

So I made a decision to get back my focus and personal power. I had done it in the past and I could do it again.

As I had heard often in the past, "Ask the question enough times and the answers will come."

I have gone from loving the web as a personal research tool, to building my very own website. I still stop and shake my head that I have done this. I chose my domain name www.law-of-attraction-success-secrets.com, because I totally believe in the Law of Attraction. Yet there is so much more to getting the life you really want than know this Law. This is one of the many fantastic "power of the mind" techniques you can use to eliminate the blockages in your life to set you on the path you really deserve. These techniques are not just New Age rhetoric, but powerful change strategies.

It is so exciting. I run teleclasses and provide personal coaching on different topics that all revolve around eliminating the sabotage and creating massive focus in people's lives. It doesn't matter whether your blockages are manifesting themselves as money issues, poor health or shaky relationships, the change strategies are much the same.

My business is growing and developing and every turn in the road is exciting. This has only happened because I once again fired up my focus and became razor sharp on what I really did want.

I know a lot of people don't do what they really want because they are afraid, but you can remove that fear. There are simple techniques available to you. Don't go to your grave wishing you had done this or that. Just take a leap of faith and do it. Sometimes just being prepared to fail takes away the fear.

I practice what I preach, but I am not perfect. In the past when I noticed something was not working, I would spend far too much time trying to force results and change. Now when I notice things are not happening as I wish, I stop, go to a quiet place, and work on myself. I know the blockages are coming from within and so will the answers.

I love what I am doing, and you will probably have heard this before, but I think it is one of the real keys to success.

I have a post it note on my computer that says "How many peoples' lives have you enhanced today." I often look at it and on some days I can answer lots of people, and it is so exciting. Then on other days the only life I have enhanced is my own and you know what, that is enough.

Trish Riedel has spent the majority of her life studying the wonders of human behavior, attempting to understand how some people easily succeed while others don't. Trish became a certified NLP Practitioner more than 10 years ago. She has combined a range of ideas and concepts to develop an effective change strategy.

Join her free Teleclasses and sign up for her free eBook "*7 Tips for Success*" by registering at www.Law-Of-Attraction-Success-Secrets.com.

Go "Green" and Get Healthy Pink Skin

Vivienne Hill

Pretty much from my first bottle-fed slurps, I developed a nasty skin disease called eczema. It was an uncomfortable, crazily itchy and sometimes downright painful condition that meant I must wear bandages or gloves to bed for my first year of life. I was born in the closing days of the 1950s in England, in that still almost post war period when all medicines were considered great developments. General thoughts were if it was made in a laboratory, it was probably superior to any product nature could provide. So liberal applications of steroid creams were applied to my newborn delicate redness, but they did little for my skin in the short term and nothing for it in the long run. As it was the conventional medical treatment and everyone trusted their general practitioners and dermatologists blindly, it was continued. Sometimes the eczema was so bad that it would crack and bleed. Because it was itchy I would scratch it and make it worse, hence leading to the bedtime bandaging. It was a pretty miserable disease and was embarrassing to suffer, as people seemed keen to offer either advice or disgusted glances. Both were unhelpful and just exacerbated my agony.

Life continued. The family emigrated from England to Australia in 1967 where it was hoped the skin problem would be resolved or that I would just grow out of it. So I found myself on endless sweltering summer weekends at the beach too scared to go into the water. I had found out that to enter the salt water with my eczematous rash was literally rubbing salt into the wound. The water was eventually so tempting I had to do dive in to cool down. Ouch!

Fast forward through the years back to England when I was studying for my degree. Far from disappearing as hoped, the eczema had moved from the flexures (groin and insides of my elbows) to my hands. I now had to wear white cotton gloves, or more usually only one on my left hand due to the mass of cracked bleeding rash on my fingers. I would bend my fingers and the blood would come through the glove. I still think Michael Jackson may have taken the idea of wearing one glove from me.

The birth of my third daughter in Australia in 1998 heralded a time of accelerated change in my life. I had been a practicing pharmacist for a decade and a half and while I still suffered with eczema (I was 38 years old), I had long given up going to GPs and dermatologists. I knew exactly what I would be prescribed and knew from experience it was not going to cure the eczema. Also I had learned through my studies and been told endlessly there was no cure for this disease.

Suddenly a light bulb went on in my brain! I cannot recall a specific event that lead to this enlightenment, but I decided there certainly must be a way forward and indeed I was going to cure this disease. I started thinking about things that we as a society give little heed to.

Chemicals. In my house, in my body, in my environment.

It was ironic that here I was doling out chemicals for a living and suddenly I was preparing to wage a sort of home front campaign against them. First went the washing machine detergent with the fancy 'whitening' enzymes. These powders also leave behind a very highly perfumed scent which common sense told me was probably not the best thing to be sleeping in or wearing daily. As a pharmacist I knew a huge percentage of cases of skin rashes appearing out of the blue can be attributed to people changing detergents containing those pesky little enzymes.

Then out went the food with preservatives. Canned foods were generally not so bad, but fresh and organic was better. As I thought more deeply about this change, I also embraced the idea that the planet would be rewarded for my saying no to using pesticides and chemicals in general. Organic means so much more than pesticide-free growth, but that was my main focus at the time. Thus started a whole different way of eating for the family.

Next were the 'household chemicals.' Are they called that so that people think they are harmless? Well, they all went out too. I pared the cleaning down to a simple process. We now use Enjo cleaning cloths designed to be used with water only.

I was gradually removing our chemical burden, in and around the home at least, which is where I was spent much of my time.

I then decided to utilize long (almost) forgotten cream-making skills and started making my own creams and lotions. The creams were made without preservatives and would keep in the refrigerator for a week. Using the healing properties of essential oils blended into grapeseed, jojoba and other wonderful carrier oils, saw the start of Heaven Scent Aromatherapy, my small but ethically run business. I no longer make the creams to sell, but have expanded the offerings to include handmade soaps and other products. These soaps containing essential oils for healing and clay for colour are excellent treatment bars for the skin.

Of course what you want to know is how all this affected my skin. Within a few months of removing the chemicals, all my eczema had disappeared. I occasionally had a small spot appear on a leg or arm, but it went away again within a few days. When I was pregnant with my fourth daughter, I had a recurrence of the eczema on the ring finger of my left hand, but after my daughter was born, it went away.

I had found my own cure for my 38 year skin disease by changing my life and my environment. I had scrutinized my way of living at a fundamental physical level. Change may sometimes be a bit difficult to come to terms with, and in my situation my whole family had to undergo what was to prove a quantum change in our use of chemicals. My life was changed considerably as you can imagine. I was finally free from this horrendous burden. The journey was hard, but the rewards made it all worthwhile.

Or was it the decision I had made to no longer suffer from this dis-ease? Whatever it was, my mind had been made up to improve it and the combination of positive action and thoughts lead to a cure.

Since then, I have left pharmacy behind and moved into alternative healing therapies.

Life is so full of joy, excitement and adventure. Never let go of your dreams and don't let people fool you, even if they are the 'experts' into thinking anything is impossible. Just focus and make it happen. If I can do it then so can you!

Vivienne Hill trained as a pharmacist before moving into alternative healing therapies using Bach Flower Essences, Reiki, Angelic Healing, Laughter therapy and Past Life hypnotherapy. Her handmade soaps and balms are wonderful. She loves to teach her inspiring and fun workshops on soap-making, health and happiness through personal empowerment.

Visit www.VivienneHill.com for dates of workshops or to book consultations, and get FREE simple, easy practical tips and other downloadable information and products. www.HeavenScentAromatherapy.com.

I Allowed Myself to Dream

Tracey Lunniss

My journey began 38 years ago. I came from your typical welfare, dysfunctional family. I had particular statements ingrained into me from an early age, such as "You have to work hard for money," and "People like us don't have money," that I believed it to be so.

Through various opportunities which I always took, I was lucky to be given an apprenticeship at 16, and after working long hours I managed to get myself educated at University. My driving force has always been that I love my job and now I am running my own company doing the same work and still loving it.

It has been a rough ride, but I always climbed up to the next rung of the ladder through sheer hard work and determination. My motivation in recent years has been to provide an amazing life for my family and to be able to travel and give them as many experiences as I can, along with a good education and a beautiful home.

About two years ago I attracted some really amazing people in my life. At the time I did not know why we had formed this great friendship, but knew that we were all on the same spiritual level.

My business was growing steadily, but I was working 18 hours a day. The only time I took off was to pick up my girls from school and then I would start working again once they were in bed. My debts were large mainly do to the lack of cash flow, clients having not paid on time but bills still had to be paid. The company was the only source of income.

I dreaded getting mail and was always so scared to go shopping as I did not know which credit card would be able to handle the grocery bill. I became very good at making excuses to the check out girls about why they had to try 3 or 4 different cards before finding one that didn't bounce. This is how it was and I hated it.

There was always seemed to be more money going out then was coming in, and I knew it had to change. I used to believe the harder I worked the better the situation would be. How wrong was I!!!

Roughly twelve months ago one of these new friends mentioned "The Secret," and this intrigued me.

While watching the movie, I sobbed. Deep down I knew what an amazing impact this was going to have on my life. I was not sad, but for some unknown reason I could not stop myself from crying. Something disturbed me and it was as if everything I had done in the past was done in the hardest way possible. Here was a part of a puzzle that I had not seen before and I wanted to find the rest of the pieces to make it whole.

I frantically started trying to find out what was the secret behind "The Secret." I then discovered the 'Law of Attraction,' and now wanted to know what it was and how could I work with it. I was like a bull chasing a red cloth, foaming at the mouth, knowing that I needed this so badly. I was desperate.

I was this close to dissolving the company.

It is my business to create wealth for my clients. They are all investors and I help them pay less tax from their investment properties and yet my own dream was to have my own investment properties and actually save my own taxes! I love doing what I am doing and I am really passionate about it, but I truly wanted a better lifestyle for my family.

I then started changing my thoughts. At first I would think thoughts of things that I wanted, but deep down I still had the belief, 'Tracey, you won't get that.' Nothing changed until I started thinking about what I truly wanted with emotion. It took a while to be able to do this.

I started to think about the things I would love to attract in my life when I was in a happy state. When I felt a positive emotion, I allowed myself to think of what I truly wanted, what would make my heart sing.

When I heard a song on the radio that made me feel happy, I let myself think of something that I truly would like to obtain. I would sing in my head 'Wouldn't it be nice to ......,' and I would list in my head all the things that it would be nice to have.

After six months of doing my affirmations, reading, listening and putting into practice everything I read and heard, I started to notice changes. Within six months my credit cards had been paid off, and the business started taking off in a way that was unimaginable.

Now, 12 months later, the business has grown from covering a small area in one state in Australia, to covering all the capital cities in the country. These changes have been brought about because I changed my awareness and my thoughts.

I can't say that I still don't panic and have negative thoughts because I do, but I don't dwell on them. To stop focusing on the problems/negative thoughts, I would get a book out and start reading or listen to an audio, one that changes my feelings, until I start to focus again on the positive thoughts.

Having shifted my thought patterns, I now let myself feel grateful for everything I have or experience. When I am going through issues with my husband, I look at things that I am 'grateful for' in him. It may be the fact that I know he loves me, so then I become grateful for his love. This then takes me away from the negative feelings and I start to experience positive thoughts once more.

Recently, I have taken my family overseas, have acquired investment properties, and bought my dream car. My whole life has been transformed; my dreams are coming to fruition.

Why am I telling you this, you may ask? It's not about how well I am doing - it's about how I changed my way of thinking and turned my whole life around and changed my beliefs in such a short time frame.

If you change your mindset and your thoughts, you can then have whatever you dream, as long as you give your true emotions to your thoughts. You need to really focus your thoughts with passion on what you really want to bring it about.

I don't work those long hours anymore either. I work smarter and I take time to dream. I now remember that I can dream, and have given myself permission to do so.

I now know that I don't have to struggle to achieve my dreams. I have put that stage of my life behind me and I am so looking forward to designing my future. My future is very exciting and I can't wait to see what I attract into my life next.

I was once told that success does not bring happiness. I have actually found that happiness brings success.

Just remember to dream.

Tracey Lunniss is a mother, Chartered Quantity Surveyor, entrepreneur & apprentice dream attractor. Tracey derives great satisfaction from helping her clients become financially independent by achieving the maximum benefits from their property investments.

To receive your free report, '*The 7 Vital Facts You Should Know About Property Depreciation*', please visit www.TSLProjectServices.com.au. For support and guidance on being a landlord please visit www.LandlordSpecialists. com.au or contact Tracey at Tracey@TSLProjectServices.com.au, www.TraceyLunniss.com, or via telephone at +61 7 3806 2986.

Overcome Metabolic Syndrome and Lose Weight Permanently

Gosia Kuszewski

S truggle with weight? Feel tired and crave sugary foods? Perhaps Metabolic Syndrome could be your problem.

If you battle with your weight, it is very possible that you may have an underlying problem called Metabolic Syndrome which causes all kinds of misery. In order to deal with problems such as tiredness, sugar cravings or poor concentration, you need to understand the causes of Metabolic Syndrome.

The questionnaire below lists the most common symptoms of Metabolic Syndrome:

1. Do you store weight around your waist?

   (Females above 35 inches (88 cm), Males above 40 inches (102cm)

2. Do you struggle with your weight despite watching what you eat?

3. Do you crave sugary or starchy foods?

4. Do you have poor memory and concentration?

5. Do you feel tired all the time?

6. Do you have high blood cholesterol?

7. Do you have high blood pressure?

8. Do you have a history of heart disease or diabetes?

If you answered "yes" to more than 3 of those questions, there is a great chance you may have it.

The problem which lies behind all those symptoms is Insulin Resistance (Metabolic Syndrome or Syndrome X). Trouble with insulin begins when your body becomes resistant to this hormone which controls blood sugar levels. Insulin in excessive amounts stores fat, causes cravings, increases heart disease, the incidence of diabetes and elevates blood pressure.

Excess refined carbohydrates, sugars and saturated fats all cause insulin resistance. Also stress, genetics, lack of muscle, and carrying excess fat around the waist are contributing factors as well.

The good news is that Insulin Resistance and its effects can be completely reversed by following a simple eating plan, correcting digestive function and with key nutrients supplements.

The quickest and most effective way to correct this problem, lose weight and dismiss cravings forever, is to limit the amount of processed carbohydrates and sugars in your diet.

Overeating carbohydrates can prevent a higher percentage of fats from being used for energy, which leads to an increase in fat storage. Your body has a limited ability to store excess carbohydrates, and it will convert them into body fat. Refined carbohydrates stimulate the production of insulin much more than complex carbohydrates do.

Initially, it is best to completely avoid bread, cereals, pasta, rice, cookies, sweets, alcohol, soft drinks and juices. Later on you can include small amounts of rye bread or brown rice back into your daily diet. Refined carbohydrates require little or no digestion and provoke excessive insulin production, leaving you tired, hungry, irritable, and unable to concentrate.

Instead try including small but frequent protein meals in your diet, as protein is crucial to help reverse Insulin Resistance. It not only balances blood sugar levels, it also rebuilds cellular tissue and promotes muscle growth.

Portion size is also very important. Even if you eat insulin friendly foods, a large meal can still provoke a high insulin response. It is much better to eat 4 – 5 small meals a day than consume 2 – 3 large ones.

How our digestion affects insulin

Digestive problems are a hidden cause of Insulin Resistance. This is because 70% of the body's immunity is located in the stomach. If you have food intolerances such as wheat or dairy sensitivity, your system has to constantly battle with processing these foods which interrupts the function of insulin. Also the presence of organisms such as Candida albicans, unfriendly bacteria, parasites and worms, cause pollution within your digestion putting stress on your immune system. Symptoms like bloating, heartburn, constipation or diarrhea, and indigestion are examples of some of the digestive symptoms affecting the proper balance of insulin. Diets high in sugar and processed foods also contribute to the overgrowth of bad bacteria and yeast.

Is there anything else to speed up the process of reversing Metabolic Syndrome?

There are number of nutrients which help to reverse Metabolic Syndrome as follows:

- Chromium helps to balance blood sugar and stabilize insulin levels.

- Magnesium supports insulin function and helps to produce energy.

- Calcium burns fat and neutralizes acid in your body.

- Zinc is a key mineral regulating insulin function and also promotes enzyme production for better digestion.

- Good fats, like fish oils and flaxseed oil, help to balance blood sugar and regulate insulin levels.

- Antioxidants also play a key role in protecting cell membranes from damage which can lead to insulin resistance.

- Digestive herbs like Black Walnut, Wormwood, Gentian, Ginger, Garlic, Thyme, Pau D'Arco, help to eliminate bad bacteria and improve digestion, absorption and elimination.

Exercise is another important factor. The more you do, the faster you see results. When exercising, your insulin balances, so keep moving.

Building muscle will improve your metabolic rate and also slows down ageing.

What should we eat to balance sugar levels and stabilize insulin?

The following suggestions have been tested by hundreds of people with fantastic results. They are simple, easy and delicious. Try them and the results will amaze you.

Eating suggestions to balance insulin and blood sugar levels:

- Have up to 4 cups of vegetables per day. (Avoid potatoes and corn).

- Eat around 1 palm-sized portion (100 grams) of protein a day. Example: 2 eggs for breakfast, 100g fish for lunch, 120g chicken for dinner.

- Snack on nuts or seeds like a handful of almonds, sunflower or pumpkin seeds.

- Eat no more than 2 pieces of fruit per day. Preferably berries, cherries, grapefruit, or honeydew melon.

- Limit dairy products to 2 -3 times a week (low fat cottage cheese, feta, ricotta, sour cream, plain yogurt).

- Drink plenty of water, green tea, herbal teas.

- Add flaxseed oil and apple cider vinegar to your salads as a dressing.

- Have protein at each meal and chew properly. Your last meal should be no later then 6:30 pm.

Meal suggestions (choose one):

Breakfast:
1. Omelet – 2 eggs, 3 mushrooms, half tomato.
2. Cottage cheese, tomato, sliced turkey

3. Protein shake + milk + berries
4. Ground seeds (linseed, sunflower, pumpkin, sesame, almonds with yogurt + strawberries

Lunch:
1. Can of tuna or salmon, salad, olives, feta cheese, tomatoes, salad dressing made of flaxseed and apple cider vinegar.
2. Zucchini Quiche

Dinner:
1. Grilled salmon and stir fried veggies.
2. Steak with salad.
3. Chicken soup with veggies (see our website for more recipes)

Let's face it; carbohydrates are addictive so it takes time to change your taste and habits. The benefits of this eating plan are profound and sustainable. Remember, initially you need to be very strict and focused, but once you lose weight and balance your insulin, it will be much easier. Your energy will increase and cravings will diminish.

If you fall off the wagon, do not despair or lose inspiration. Just get back into a healthy eating plan, read motivational books, quotes and get inspired listening to CD's. Get in contact with positive people who are exercising on a regular basis, so they can inspire you. Don't allow anyone to sabotage your weight loss efforts, stay focused and determined. There is no better feeling then being slim and radiant with energy.

Hundreds of my clients were able to do it, so can you! Here's to your success!

Gosia Kuszewski practices Naturopathy with great enthusiasm and passion. She lives what she teaches, has a positive outlook on life and takes care of her wellbeing to the fullest capacity. She loves to inspire and motivate others, and encourages them to take control of their health. Born in Poland, she now lives with her two beautiful daughters in Australia. For more information and recipes, visit Gosia's website at www.SunshineCoastWeightLossCentre.com.au or email her at Info@ SunhineCostWeightLossCentre.com.au.

THE POWER IN LIVING FOR YOURSELF

Gail Harris

You are who the world has been waiting for.

Have you ever thought that you wanted to make a real difference in this world? You know, do something amazing that would make this planet a better place for you having been here? I know that I have had this niggling desire my entire conscious life and my guess is that everyone has some longing for a different and better world, but hey, where to start?

This is my story about where to start.

It is a story about you and how you are already making a difference, whether you realize it or not.

It's about your incredible power and ability to not only create the life you desire, but how you are also uniquely contributing to the evolution of humanity and life everywhere, every minute of every day.

This is a story about the energetics of life.

It is a story about the connectedness of everything across space and time!

You will see how this invisible intertwining, can create a life of limitless possibilities, when you understand how to use your power with conscious intent.

Imagine a world where everyone knew how to source life from this place, what an incredibly exciting thought.

And so, this is also a story about hope.

Hope for yourself, your children, their children and a future of our own conscious creation where anything is possible!!

Sounds incredible? You are incredible!

It's true you know. We are all incredible, in a way that may not be obvious, so come with me as we explore the power source of life itself and the amazing contribution everyone of us is making.

Let's begin with a little background information, for even though we have all been part of evolution, you may forget how you actually participated. A cool thought huh?

Have you ever thought how evolution occurs? I mean the evolution of humanity, the big stuff! Why is life so different now than say a hundred years ago, fifty years ago, even ten? Who has created all this change and how did it actually come to be? For, it is only in knowing how it actually occurred, that we can do anything about creating the type of evolution we would all like to put our name to. This is an ongoing process and now is the time for us to start doing this evolutionary thing in a conscious way.

So, let's begin with you and what calls you to the next step in your life.

If you look at history, you can see that the vision and passion to create something new has always been the source of the next movement. It feels like life is always pulling us into our next creation, which in turn becomes our new reality. History books are full of men and women, who very consciously followed this call from within and lived their lives from their vision of a new possibility. They took on the big questions and helped evolve them into a new reality.

Questions like:

What if we could fly?

What if we could be free to say what we wanted?

What if we could move mountains and build amazing structures?

What if?

What if?

You see, it is going on all the time and you are part of it. Just look around you and everything, absolutely everything, was at one point a mere thought. A thought that gained momentum and lead you in a pathway of creation. You know the feeling. An idea starts to bubble; you create a vision of 'what if' and a new possibility develops and begins to evolve.

When you focus on an outcome that is full of 'passionate wanting', the energy builds and moves you into inspired thought and action. Your life is on the move in a deliberate and conscious way. You begin to interact with the unseen aspect of life, the 'energetics' and your life begins to flow.

Sometimes we call it 'luck' or 'coincidence', but really, you are responsible for all of it. It feels great when you live in your power and life turns out exactly how you intended it to.

Just reflect on all the amazing relationships, circumstances and things that make up your life and you will see how incredible you are! And when you question why all areas of your life are not as you desire, think about the beliefs and visions that you hold for yourself in relation to these particular areas.

Upon reflection, you will recognize that certain beliefs do not support your vision and what you are really wanting for your next life experience. In other words, you don't think that you can get what you want, and so this becomes your resistance. Your movement forward will only occur once you choose to be the power and not give it away to your limiting beliefs.

Power is sourced from within every single one of us, in exactly the same way. You have a vision for your day, week, year, the world and for some, even humanity. When you are in alignment with this vision and sourcing life from this place, then you will notice the ease in which your life begins to flow. We are all on a constant path of creation, in both a conscious and unconscious way.

So, let's stop for a minute, get in touch with this power and consciously experience our ability to create!

Sit or stand in a balanced and comfortable way and focus your attention on your breathing. Notice when you do this, how your consciousness is focused within your body and you experience its' movement with each breath.

Now, expand your consciousness out beyond your body in every direction, out to the edges of the room, or even further if you wish.

Begin to play, fill the space with joy and lightness and then notice how you feel. Amp it up a little more and connect with your passion, you know that place where your heart and mind are aligned and you can't stop smiling. Oh, what a wonderful energy passion is!

Now, fill it with love and beauty and notice the impact in your body. Your choices are limitless, so let yourself explore whatever takes your fancy, noticing how each new intention brings with it a whole new experience.

Your power, quite simply, lies in your ability to create the energetics that you desire. And because we are energetic beings, living in a vibrational world, what we draw into our lives is always a vibrational match to what we have created.

You expand your energy out beyond your physical form every day, affecting and contributing to the energetics of the whole and to the experience of those around you.

Imagine a world where everyone was conscious of the energy that they were creating. Imagine a world where everyone knew that they were contributing to the collective energy of everything and the evolution of humanity.

Do you think that this would change the way they lived their lives?

I know that the power is with every single one of us. How simple is that and what a great place to start making a difference.

It's true you know, you are incredible, we all are!

Gail Harris is a Teacher, Life Coach and founder of Education for Living. She is a passionate explorer of human potential and her commitment is to inspire and support powerful conscious living in every individual. For further information she can be contacted at GailHarris15@optusnet.com.au or visit her website at www.YouAreWhotheWorldisWaitingFor.com.

How HABITS Really Work

Jack Canfield, Mark Victor Hansen and Les Hewitt

Your Habits Will Determine Your Future

What is a habit? Simply stated, a habit is something you do and often it becomes easy. In other words, it's a behavior that you keep repeating. If you persist at developing a new behavior, eventually it becomes automatic.

For example, if you learn to drive a car with a standard gearshift, the first few lessons are usually interesting. One of the big challenges is figuring out how to synchronize the clutch and accelerator pedals to so you have a nice, smooth gear change. If you release the clutch too quickly, the car stalls. If you press down too hard on the accelerator without releasing the clutch, the engine roars but you don't go anywhere. Sometimes the car jumps down the street like a kangaroo, surging and stopping as the new driver struggles with the pedals. However, with practice, the gear change eventually becomes smooth and you don't think about it anymore.

The great news is that you can reprogram yourself any time you choose to do so! If you're struggling financially, this is important to know!

Let's say you want to be financially independent. Doesn't it make sense to check your money making habits? Are you in the habit of paying yourself first every month? Do you consistently save and invest at least 10 percent of your income? The answer is either "yes" or "no." Immediately you can see if you are moving in the right direction. The key word here is *consistent*. That means every month. And every month is a good habit. Most people dabble when it comes to growing their money. They are very inconsistent.

Suppose you start a savings and investment program. For the first six months you diligently put your 10 percent away according to plan.

Then something happens. You borrow the money to take a vacation, and you tell yourself you'll make it up in the next few months. Of course you don't – and your financial independence program is stalled before it even gets off the ground! By the way, do you know how easy it is to become financially secure? Starting at age eighteen if you invest one hundred dollars per month compounding annually at ten percent, you will have more than $1.1 million tucked away at age sixty-five. Even if you don't start until you are forty years old, there's hope, although it will take more than a daily dollar to do it.

This is called a **no exception policy**. In other words, you commit to your better financial future every single day. It's what separates the people who have from the people who don't have. (In chapter 9, Taking Decisive Action, you'll learn a lot more about wealth creation.)

Let's look at another situation. If maintaining excellent health is high on your list of priorities, exercising three times a week may be the minimum standard to keep you in shape. A No Exceptions Policy means you will maintain this exercise habit no matter what happens, because you value the long term benefits.

People who dabble at change will quit after a few weeks or months. And they usually have a long list of excuses why it didn't work out for them. **If you want to distance yourself from the masses and enjoy a unique lifestyle, understand this – your habits will determine your future.**

It's that important. Remember, successful people don't drift to the top. It takes focused action, personal discipline and lots of energy every day to make things happen. The habits you develop from this day forward will ultimately determine how your future works out. Rich or poor. Healthy or unhealthy. Fulfilled or unfulfilled. Happy or unhappy. It's your choice, so choose wisely.

Your Habits Will Determine Your Quality Of Life

Many people today are concerned about their lifestyle. Phrases like, "I'm looking for a better quality of life," or "I just want to simplify my life," are now commonplace. It seems the headlong rush for material success and all the trappings of a so-called successful life are not enough. To be truly rich includes not only financial freedom, but developing rich, meaningful relationships, enriching your health, and enjoying a rich balance between your career and your personal life.

The nourishment of your own spirit or soul is also an essential requirement. This takes time to explore and expand. It is a never ending process. The more you learn about yourself – how you think, how you feel, what your true purpose is and how you want to live – the more your life will flow.

Instead of just working hard every week, you will begin to make better choices based on intuition and instinctively knowing the right thing to do. It is this higher level of awareness that determines your daily quality of life. In chapter 10, Living On Purpose, we'll show you a unique system that will make all of this possible for you. It's a very exciting way to live.

The Results Of Your Bad Habits Usually Don't Show Up Until Much Later In Life

Please make sure you are really alert before you read the next two paragraphs. If you're not, go splash some cold water on your face so you will not miss the importance of this fundamental concept.

More people than ever are living for immediate gratification. They buy things they can't really afford and put off payment as far down the road as possible. Cars, furniture, appliances, entertainment systems, or the latest "toy," just to name a few. People in the habit of doing this have a sense of playing catch-up all the time. There's always another payment next month. This often results in working longer hours or taking an additional job just to make ends meet, creating even more stress.

Taken to an extreme. If your expenses constantly exceed your income, you will have an ultimate outcome. It's called bankruptcy! When you develop a chronic bad habit, life will eventually give you consequences. And you may not like the consequences. Here's what you need to really understand: Life will still give you the consequences. Whether you like it or not isn't the issue. The fact is, if you keep on doing things a certain way you will always get a predictable result. **Negative habits breed negative consequences. Successful habits create positive rewards.** That's just the way life is.

Let's look at a few other examples. If you want to enjoy longevity, you must have healthy habits. Practicing good nutrition, exercising and studying longevity play a major role here. The reality? Most of the population in the Western world is overweight, under-exercised and undernourished. How would you explain that? Again, it's a live-for-the-moment attitude, with little or no thought given to future consequences. There's a long list when it comes to health. Here are a couple – working fourteen hours a day seven days a week will lead to eventual burnout. When you're eating fast foods or junk food on the run as a daily habit, the combination of stress and high cholesterol produces a much greater risk of heart attacks and strokes. These are life-threatening consequences, yet many people ignore the obvious and roll merrily along, undaunted by the fact that a major crisis may be looming just around the corner.

Look at relationships. Marriage is in trouble, with almost 50 percent ending up in divorce. If you are in the habit of starving your most important relationships of time, energy and love, how can you expect a happy outcome?

When it comes to money, your bad habits may lead you to a never-ending cycle of work in your later years, when you'd rather be enjoying more time off for fun.

Now here's some really good news:

YOU CAN TURN NEGATIVE CONSEQUENCES INTO POSITIVE REWARDS...
Simply By Changing Your Habits Now!

———————————

Jack Canfield, Mark Victor Hansen, and Les Hewitt, "Your Habits Will Determine Your Future" from *The Power of Focus: How to Hit Your Business, Personal and Financial Targets with Absolute Certainty.* Copyright 2000 by Jack Canfield, Mark Victor Hansen and Les Hewitt. Reprinted with the permission of Health Communications Inc., www.cibooks.com.

A Vision is the Key to
Having the Life You Desire

Brigitte Zonta

I was a school drop out. I didn't enjoy school. I knew there was something bigger and better out there and I knew I wasn't going to get it at school. At 15, I decided to leave (with the advice of the principal to consider another option rather than traditional schooling). I ventured out into the 'real world' not knowing what I wanted to do.

I tried numerous things after leaving school. Working at a local law firm I quickly realized that making coffee and doing the filing was not going to make me happy, nor was it very satisfying. I was surrounded by people that had no future vision, were metaphysically heavy and had dreams they thought were unreachable. Soon I found myself with the same disease as the rest of my peers. I started to think that life was all too hard and that I just had to get through one day at a time.

I managed to stay employed at a local store while my peers were unemployed, homeless and most on illegal substances. At the time I didn't think anything of it, but after being around so much negativity, I slowly found myself in a destructive and violent relationship. My whole life seemed to be washed with sadness; it was dark, scary and cold there. You could easily see it when you looked in my eyes. The sparkle I once had was gone and a dull gaze seemed to replace it. The bounce in my step was no longer there; my legs and feet dragged heavily wherever I walked. A short time ago I was happy; now I had invisible shackles upon my feet. Feeling suffocated and trapped, I could no longer take long deep breaths to fill my lungs, shallow empty breaths took their place. As I closed my eyes at night, I wished the monster I lay next to would go away. With every night came a nightmare of screams and fights. I tried to leave many times. The master plan was that I stay with my partner and make it through the very hard times. Under the cloud of sadness that floated above my head, I seemed to disappear.

Through the treacherous years of physical, emotional and psychological abuse, I managed to become a mother. It was at that point I found a reason to live. A slight shimmer of light returned to my eyes, as right then I knew I had to take responsibility for what was happening in my world. I didn't know how, but deep inside my heart I knew I could do something and I had to take action now!

The results for the university entrance test came - "ACCEPTED" was all I saw. Excitement filled my body, my eyes filled with tears and I embraced my son as I cried. I thanked God, as now I had a vision of what freedom might look like. As I painted this picture in my head, it felt so right. I had butterflies in my stomach and the hairs on my arms stood on end. I felt a lump in my throat and the rush of my heart. I knew if I focused I would get what I wanted.

My first semester started. I was finally there. Designer clothes wrapped my body, a smile on my face. The world was ignorant to my situation, the pain that I felt and the hurt as I walked. Bruises covered my body and tears filled my eyes. I was scared and alone, but my vision was still in my heart. My throat was tight and my chest heavy, my breathing was shallow and slight. I was ready to start my journey - a new step to freedom - a new step for a new life.

I wasn't sure what I was going to study, but knew it was the right place for me. I slowly started to gain interest in subjects of Psychology. I was learning more and more about myself, the world, being a parent and my destructive relationship. I focused on my studies, my son and always kept that vision in my mind. Every night as I went home to the heat of hell, my vision and my son were the only heaven among it all.

Over the next four years through the abuse and neglect, I finally found who I was. I attended many personal development seminars, my self-esteem and confidence increased in leaps and bounds. During my third year of university I realized that I played a part in my destructive situation. After discovering the principals of the Law of Attraction, I discovered that the only thing I had been focusing on was how badly he treated me. It was time to change my mindset. My old patterns were broken as well as my partners. We tried to work it out again, one more time, .We promised to only focus on what we wanted. We realized we had spent our whole ten years together focusing on what we didn't want and what we didn't have.

I finally completed my university degree with a distinction average. I remember standing proud and consumed with joy, smiling from ear to ear. My parents cried as they watched, memories running through their minds of how their daughter had to grow. My partner who was once the monster who put invisible shackles around my feet, had also grown with me over the years, stood proudly next to me. He now showers me with love and adores me every step of my way. My new vision was forming.

I knew the man I would attract in my life would be caring, understanding and fun. This was what I found myself focusing on, and finally this was how my partner became. I was already living with the man I dreamed of, I just hadn't allowed him to be. As I sit here now and reminisce, I have gone from unreachable dreams to living the life I desire. I always knew I would teach others the tools I used to move forward, so they can have what their hearts desire as well. Whether it's an amazing relationship, having better rapport with clients and staff members or creating a plentiful amount of riches I help them find a way. By working through personal patterns and limitations we can break any old pattern and allow new ones to form. Anyone can change it just takes effort, time and a precise vision to get where you want to go.

Now I spend my days doing what I love at a space I call the The Health Hut (www.thehealthhut.com.au). Knowing that I started with no education, no money, no support, no love and no real idea about what I was going to do, only a vision in my mind. By focusing and being consistent with my visualization and affirmations I have now been able to create the life I have always dreamed of. It doesn't matter what challenges we go through, we must remember they are only temporary. Nothing is ever permanent, it can change. If you focus, are consistent and work towards what you want, you will create it. I did!

Brigitte Zonta is a Personal Development Consultant with extensive training in Psychology and NLP (Neuro-linguistic Programming). She lives an affluent life with her sons, Zane and Hunter and husband of 12 years Mick. Brigitte offers private or online consultations and runs workshops on many topics ranging from self-development to improving relationships.

Brigitte can be contacted via email at Brigitte@MakingWomenStronger.com or by phone in Sydney, Australia on 02 9754 2456. Alternatively, visit her website at www.MakingWomenStronger.com.

NEVER GIVE UP ON LOVE

Diana Cribb

My life has been a constant succession of coincidences. So many, and so often, that I can no longer ignore the fact that I am being guided. I may have thought I was in control, but it is very evident that a Being with a greater intellect that I could ever aspire to, and a greater purpose that I can only guess at, has carefully choreographed every step I have taken. All I know is that this mapping of my life is for the greater good of mankind. Consequently, I must bow to this Being's higher intellect and intent.

For the first five years of my life, I was happy. We lived on a farm where I could laugh, sing, and shout frequently, without disturbing anyone. The only challenge I had was that I appeared to see and hear things that other people did not. Needless to say, I found this a bit confusing. If I told my parents about what I had seen or heard, they would say I must not talk like that or I would be put into a mental institution. I did not know what a mental institution was at the time, but I did know it did not sound very nice. It became clear to me that my own reality was not quite the same as everyone else's. I could not reason why this was, so I tried not to talk to anyone unless absolutely necessary.

Once I started school, it became very obvious that I had learning difficulties. I could not follow what the teacher was trying to explain in class, and no one seemed to understand why. It was like hearing a different language spoken for the first time, without anyone present to translate it for me. I was totally lost and became very temperamental. I lived in fear of the teacher because she would stand behind me and ram the sharp end of a pencil into the top of my head whenever I didn't respond as she wanted. The remainder of the class time, I would spend standing in a waste paper basket in the corner. I preferred this punishment, as I was at least safe from attack by the teacher.

By the time I left school, I was illiterate and innumerate. I had managed to learn to read, albeit very poorly, with the help of a retired schoolteacher who lived in a village two miles away. She was very kind to me, and realized I wasn't simply being just difficult. I finally was diagnosed as being dyslexic when I was eighteen, a little too late for an academic career. This started my adventure for self-improvement, which I am continuing with today. Yet I still continue to hear and see differently than most people.

Do you believe in love at first sight? Well, it is real and it happened to me. We met at a school firework night. I could only see his face in the light of a bonfire. He said "Hello, my name is Preston Cribb." I fell head over heels in love in that instant, and have never recovered. You may think we got married and lived happily ever after. Not so, as it took us some forty plus years before we finally got our act together and got married. We had one of those stupid teenage quarrels that culminated in us going our separate ways, however, we managed to remain friends.

As a teenager, Preston was always playing jokes on my mother. He would write his name in the dust to see how long it would take before she cleaned. One day, my mother was dusting a favorite picture of hers and found he had signed it. She could not see how, as it was sealed inside a glass frame, which had not been opened. When Preston came to see me that night, my outraged mother confronted him, telling him he had gone too far. In reply, Preston just said that it was his grandfathers' work, who was a well-known artist, and for whom he had been named after. Was it just a coincidence that my mother had owned the picture long before our friendship began?

Years later, a lady told me the village she lived in had been the venue for illegal bare knuckle boxing. The reason this village had been chosen was geographical. It was under the jurisdiction of Northamptonshire, which was sixty miles away, and by the time the sheriff was fetched to stop a boxing match, the fight was over and everyone had gone home. I told this lady that my childhood sweetheart was a descendent of Tom Cribb, the last legal world champion bare knuckle boxer, and on hearing this, she asked me if I would like to meet him. I thought this was a bit odd, as Tom Cribb had lived in the eighteenth century. She then produced a very old picture of him and asked if my friend would like to have it. I said he would love it.

Years went by, and we both married other partners. My husband and I lived in England, and Preston and his wife moved to Australia. When Preston came to England to visit his mother, we would also see each other, as Preston would visit my mother as well. I think our Mums were determined to get us back together one day. Each time, I would try to find the picture of Tom Cribb to give to him, but I could never find it, almost as if it was hiding.

Some thirty years passed and both of our respective partners had passed away. While a young friend of mine was helping me clear out my attic, he called down to me that he had found an old geezer and asked if I wanted him. I was delighted as he had found the picture of Tom Cribb.

For a long time I did not tell Preston that my husband had passed away. I knew he was on his own, and I feared the outcome of us meeting again. He still lived in Australia with his family, and my family was in England. When I was told we would be together again by a clairvoyant friend of mine, I flew into a panic. We had such a turbulent relationship as teenagers, and I was terrified we would quarrel again. In the end, my niece went to see Preston and told him what had happened. Then the letter I had dreaded receiving finally arrived. He was coming to England to see me.

Our feelings for one another had never been in question; it was just whether we could live together without annihilating one another. We need not have worried, because we could not remember what we had quarreled about, anyway. Time has mellowed us.

We are married now and living in Australia, where I practice as a psychic writer and healer. My family is only a flight away, and we can talk to one another whenever we want to. The world we knew as teenagers seems to have shrunk quite a bit due to new technology, but the love that I 'saw' all those years ago has never faded.

Diana Cribb, psychic, writer, and healer, personal philosophy is, "Put your hand in God's, and go for it! You are never too old to learn." If you would like to learn more about Diana, visit her website at www.DianaCribb.com to sign up for newsletters, and free articles on, writing from God and His minions, Healing, and Tom Cribb. You can also email her at cribbintl@optusnet.com or phone at Australia 03 9877 2412.

Switch on Your Lasting Power

Tatiana Perera

I live in a lush part of Sydney with bay views and a five minute walk to a beautiful beach where I do my handstands, yoga exercises and kilometer swim. I love to splash in the surf a few times a week and go on my walks along the magnificent Bondi cliff walk where movies are made as the views are so spectacular. I enjoy going dancing and I also love scuba diving and it's a wonderful feeling to be able to please myself and go diving whenever I want, in any part of the world.

I not only like to keep fit but have a youthful body of a 30 year old at my age of over 60 years. This is all due to my high energy level that I developed and that has helped me get over a very disempowered past.

The method I teach today I learned from having to practice changing my own moods states from my early 20's as I was depressed most of the time due to my dysfunctional childhood. This was followed by a dysfunctional marriage where my husband humiliated me and created the sort drama my mother used to do. In order to get some peace in my life, at the end of my week I would meditate on Sunday mornings and I reached a wonderful peaceful state each time. My spiritual teacher would remind me that this was the state to have all the time, but I simply could never hold onto it, and back I'd come into my frustrated daily self as soon as I came out of meditation.

Shortly after I joined a multilevel marketing company, a lady arrived on the scene who continued to annoy me with her brash behavior. One day I confided my feelings to a friend who asked me how I felt when she would seemingly barge in on other people's conversations. To my surprise I discovered that secretly I wanted to be outgoing, just like this lady, but since her behavior reminded me of my mother, I had kept these internal feelings suppressed. This 'aha' moment was a real eye opener for me. Afterwards when I had integrated this truth into my life, I stopped noticing that she had once annoyed me. Many years later when our paths crossed again, with her being the client and me the facilitator, I was able to share with her how my personal growth had begun with her in those early days.

Another time when I found out that my husband had gambled all our money away and realized the $2000 limit of my credit card was all the money I had, I remember how this thought terrified me. I decided every time this thought came up, I'd switch to think about the success of my classes instead. I fought this thought each week for months! My classes would go great, but as I never knew who would turn up the following week, the panic of lack would engulf me. So I was forced to practice positive thinking all the time. What a way to learn about the Law of Attraction!

The major turning point for me was when I had to take a whole year off work and had a minor operation. I was in so much pain that I had to go on social benefits as I couldn't pay my bills. By some remarkable coincidence the "universe" put me in touch with an amazing opportunity to work overseas on a trial basis all expenses paid, just what I needed! Unfortunately the company folded and I returned home 3 months later, broke.

I realized this was a new beginning for me and decided to focus only on what truly made me happy. Keeping negative thoughts out of my head worked like a charm and I began watching my feelings and realized I alone was responsible for them. Soon afterwards my work literally took off, and when I began working with my technique in earnest everything began to flow as if my some magic.

I began to use my technique to release stagnated feelings and incorporated this into my teaching. From here, the Orgasmic Effect was born, where I recognized how easy it was to switch on and access orgasmic-like feelings, which are feelings connected to the heart. When business takes over people's lives, people generally disconnect from their heart and stress builds up. This affects relationships on all levels, and this can be when men resort to genital relief which in the long term is not satisfying.

At last I'm successfully teaching the wonderful Energy Control technique which had supported me in those early days. I teach this technique to mostly male clients as it improves their performance in the bedroom. What I'm thrilled about is I have created a fast track method in our modern day and age for men to overcome performance issues which are linked to feelings of inadequacy. Using this simple and easy method, men can not only last as long as they want to in the bedroom, but they walk out feeling happy and enthusiastic about their future relationships and experience a renewal within their marriage.

They come to me rather than go see a counselor, as most men do not want to admit that they may need this type of help.

What I love about the method I have developed is that I help men from all walks of life who struggle with their feelings of inadequacy and stress about their bedroom performance. But when they start using this simple technique, they not only succeed in the bedroom but the technique teaches them how to overcome feelings of low self-esteem in all other areas of their lives.

Sexual energy is an emotion that is activated during sexual intimacy. Gratitude, love, appreciation and acknowledgement are also emotions. If having sex can be compared to the lower notes upon the musical scale, then the other emotions like, acknowledgement, appreciation, love, gratitude could be compared to the higher notes upon the scale. We all know how important these higher emotions are and how we crave to feel them. Not getting these higher emotions such as appreciation etc. on a daily basis causes us to feel unloved and not appreciated. *What if you couldn't* get to some of these higher tender emotions due to a relationship break up or illness? What if you could learn *how to use an 'internal switch' to turn on positive emotion* that could lift or change your whole mood state for the whole day?

To give people control of their internal switch where they can turn on positive emotions any time during the day is very liberating. Rather than resorting to drink, sex or many other addictions that many men seek as alternative ways of releasing negative tension. Therefore it brings me great joy knowing that I am contributing some peace in our troubled world by bringing in this easy to use technique that can be learnt in one session.

Tatiana teaches people how to turn up their internal power, vitality and enthusiasm using their own sexual energy like a switch. This method not only allows men to be able to last longer in the bedroom, but also works equally well for healing your body and changing any life situation. "The Orgasmic Effect" is an amazing energy control method. Seminars to train therapists will be available by 2009. See how it can work for you at www.TheOrgasmicEffect.com.